Book 7 Reflections of God Moments

56 One Minute Devotionals

1

Dedication:

To those who have shown grace and beauty through their hearts to others despite their circumstances of life, I dedicate this book to mothers and all women who have abounded in grace. To my mother, Teresa, I know of no other whose wisdom and grace truly embodies this scripture. You always said if I had nothing good to say, then say nothing. I hope that these words from the Lord and through my life speak only good things.

Heart Abounding
Book 7 Reflections of God Moments
copyright © 2024

Written by: Donesa Walker
Design by: Will Baten
Edited by: Kelley Inderman

Contents

God means what he says. What he says goes. His powerful Word is sharp as a surgeon's scalpel, cutting through everything, whether doubt or defense, laying us open to listen and obey. Nothing and no one can resist God's Word. We can't get away from it—no matter what.

Hebrews 4: 12-13

The Surgeon's Tools!

I have had over 20 surgeries! I know the ropes. Each surgery is different but they all have some consistency and the one thing you want to know going in is the skill of the surgeon, because lack of skill or experience can affect outcomes. I'm not the dream candidate for surgery because I've had so many...my body is a scar filled battlefield. I never want to have surgery again as it is hard on your body, brain and everyone around you, especially me since my last few surgeries have gone sideways. However, I am not an unhealthy person nor a person who doesn't care for themselves. The bottom line is sometimes life just happens. In Hebrews, Paul sets out to demonstrate the ability of God to get to the root of our issues by comparing Him to the surgeon and His word to the scalpel a surgeon uses or in today's vernacular, a laser tool. God's word is laser focused. Paul says there is no escaping the truth of His word and no one is impervious to it. In our world where truth has taken such a hit and people manipulate everything to fit what they want things to say/be, this is refreshing. Getting to root issues is something I enjoy, surgery is not. God is purposeful in His word and in His actions. He doesn't mince words; He means them. His promises aren't just empty phrases but they have power. When we doubt His word, it doesn't stop it. It just limits our security in His promises. When we defend ourselves for poor choices, it doesn't change His mercy and grace, but we miss out on their benefits because we refuse to accept and repent. A surgeon doesn't hesitate because the body is resistant, they have an anesthesiologist give the person meds to reduce the pain and cause them to comply so they aren't resistant causing issues with movement and not disruptive during the surgery. Unfortunately, God doesn't anesthetize us before His surgeries. His actions in our lives sometimes have painful side effects. Sometimes we are willful and refuse to be quiet/still as He works on our lives. When the anesthesiologist comes in prior to surgery, he/she asks for your history and drug interactions/experience because they want to choose the best to make you comfortable so surgery is successful. But ultimately you get to choose. I'm sure most surgeons would refuse to do your surgery unless you had these meds on board because of how they know we would react to the pain of the scalpel/laser. I was awake but pain deadened for my c-sections and my lasik eye surgery. I woke up during a couple of others and I've been in a semi-awake state during others. Surgeons concentrate on what they are doing...they are laser focused because the slightest hiccup could cause the laser to go where it shouldn't.

God is our Master Healer & Great Physician. He's a Surgeon like no other. He doesn't require the anesthesia but He is thrilled when we acquiesce in Faith believing because it makes the process so much easier and the healing so much better if we are quiet and lean into His expertise. But His laser scalpel is so strong and exacting that even if we squirm and act up, He can do what He set forth to do...we just have consequences from our unwillingness to submit to His authority. Ever wonder why it seems like life is easy for others and hard for you? Well, that person you think is having it easy is probably thinking the same thing. We all have troubles. Some of us are squiggly and tenacious and things are harder for them in the process while some are just willing to allow God to work on them without all the fuss. I cannot help but remember when my two boys had their tonsils out on the same day. John was so easy. They gave him his meds, he laid there and surgery/recovery was a breeze. Gabriel on the other hand, despite the same meds, took 4 men to carry him back to surgery, tearing him from my arms and he was terrible in the whole experience. John had never had surgery. That was Gabe's third. He hadn't enjoyed any of them. They were always traumatic and recovering was tough. He knew it wasn't fun. My point is sometimes we let our previous experiences color what God is trying to work within us and instead of looking at the outcomes and good, we choose to look back at the hard recovery.
We choose to remember the struggle rather than the solution. I can say
I have had some hard surgeries for sure with rough outcomes and long healing processes.
But I can say despite the hardships, I am grateful for each one the same way I am grateful for each lesson God has sent my way through His word. Sometimes things don't go our way but God in His infinite wisdom knows us, sees us and directs us. God, help me to rest in your hands trusting that your mighty plan is enough. Let me be at peace that you have all things in your control. Let's get through these spiritual surgeries like any other with complete confidence in you.

Be anxious for nothing, but in everything by prayer and supplication, with thanksgiving, let your requests be made known to God; and the peace of God, which surpasses all understanding, will guard your hearts and minds through Christ Jesus.

I know how to be abased, and I know how to abound. Everywhere and in all things I have learned both to be full and to be hungry, both to abound and to suffer need. I can do all things through Christ who strengthens me.

And my God shall supply all your need according to His riches in glory by Christ Jesus.

Philippians 4: 6-7, 12-13, 19

Abounding While Abased!

Interesting words rarely used. Abounding is thriving and abased is its opposite which is basically struggling to make it. Paul is writing to the church at Philippi to inform them of his status and his concerns for them. He is instructive to them that your situation does not determine your future.

I've always told my students that attitude determines altitude. Attitude towards things is a small thing that makes a huge difference. The direction of your boat of life is all in how you direct your sails in the wind.
You choose to put up/take down.

You choose to allow God to work or block His moving in your life.
I've heard the saying that when life gives you lemons, you make lemonade. Well, that's a good saying but it requires living water and a little sweetness or it is still just lemon juice. Jesus says He is our source, our strength. If you are just juicing the lemons that life has given you without adding the sweetness of God's love and goodness, you will just be sour liquid to those around you. You cannot talk about living in God and refuse to allow His living water to wash your anxiety and ill away, while the expectancy of better is in your mind..,that's like refusing to add the ingredients to the lemon juice. I like lemons.

Sweet and sour is a balance I like...it's a little sassy but too much of one or the other and it's wrongly done.
When Paul spoke about abasing and abounding, his point was that he had learned, that whatever his situation, God was in it so he had learned to be at peace and trust. Life has too many ups and downs. It's like a roller coaster and you can get whiplash from the changes if you don't hold onto the steady presence of God. When you set your eyes on things above, the things below grow small and not as important. Does this mean my family and life and work are not important? Not at all. These are your places of ministry. Ministry isn't just a church thing or a mission thing...ministry is your purpose to all around you. Do they see Jesus in Your actions, words, deeds? When you are having a meltdown, who's your parent? When kids let loose, especially with tantrums, I hear parents say...see, he's all you. Well, I want people to see me at my worst and say...see, she's all God's child. This is what Paul is trying to say. In everything, EVERYTHING...good, bad, ups, downs, trials, triumphs... EVERYTHING give thanksgiving because this is the will of Christ Jesus who lives in you.

You can praise from prison and be free. You can praise in your darkest moment and find relief. Our point of praise shouldn't be determined by our emotions like it is at a ballgame. We are cheerleaders for God whether it looks like we are winning or not because we already know the ending score! Too often we let trials steal our joy and erase our security, our peace. We put our sense of wellness in the hands of people rather than the peacekeeper. God is our source.
Allow the peace of God to guard your hearts and minds. It is a choice.
I have told my boys that so much that they are tired of hearing it.

Your happiness is not determined by your circumstances or other people but rather by you! You can choose to count your blessings or your sorrows. You can choose. Choose Joy. Choose contentment, rest, peace, stillness. Let God be God and you be in His keeping. This isn't a passive place. It requires work. It requires you setting your mind ON Him, constantly. When negative thoughts come, capture them, speak His words over them. When you are exhausted, find a place of rest in your mind, heart, soul...quiet yourself and hear Him. He knows your name. He hears your heart.
Find Him. Rest in Him. Trust Him. No matter what.

You may have to do it minute by minute until it's hour by hour, then day by day, then constant.
Practice it. Lord, I trust in you!

The four living creatures, each having six wings, were full of eyes around and within. And they do not rest day or night, saying:
"Holy, holy, holy,
Lord God Almighty, Who was and is and is to come!"
"You are worthy, O Lord,
To receive glory and honor and power;
For You created all things,
And by Your will they exist and were created."

Revelation 4: 8, 11

Behold, He is coming with clouds, and every eye will see Him, even they who pierced Him. And all the tribes of the earth will mourn because of Him. Even so, Amen.
"I am the Alpha and the Omega, the Beginning and the End," says the Lord, "who is and who was and who is to come, the Almighty."

Revelation 1: 7-8

Because you have kept My command to persevere, I also will keep you from the hour of trial which shall come upon the whole world, to test those who dwell on the earth. Behold, I am coming quickly! Hold fast what you have, that no one may take your crown. He who overcomes, I will make him a pillar in the temple of My God, and he shall go out no more. I will write on him the name of My God and the name of the city of My God, the New Jerusalem, which comes down out of heaven from My God. And I will write on him My new name.

Revelation 3: 10-12

The Blessed Hope!

I love mystery novels, especially the ones with unexpected plots, twists. That's likely why I enjoy the Book of Revelation so much because it is like watching a movie unfold before me as we live in many of the last days foretold in this book. In the first 3 chapters, John has been instructed by God himself to write letters to the 7 churches. This is important as we near the time of His return, as these letters are aimed at us. The letters deliver constructive criticism and warning to most of the types of churches and promises of reward to others. In the first chapter we see the promise of His return in the clouds to catch His bride (the church) away to meet Him in the clouds.

Then He critiques the churches in chapters 2-3 leaving us with the word that those of us who are faithful until His return will not experience tribulation but will be caught away prior. Then in chapter 4, we see a glimpse of Heaven through John's eyes. I'm not going to debate biblical scholars on their interpretations here but rather focus on the "picture" of the throne room. It is a place of worship 24/7! Look at chapter 4...see the visual of winged creatures, with 100s of eyes constantly praising God....the Eagle is one...the people of America who are constantly lifting up praise...living in and dwelling in His presence-maybe the 1000s of eyes are ours or windows like our phones...what-ever...that's not the point now...the point is the praise...the portal to glory and away from your problems isn't a drug, a pain reliever or even the miracle you seek...it is PRAISE!

Oh that we could truly grasp this! Put on the garment of praise...rid ourselves of the spirit of heaviness...lift up our arms to God....pray in The Spirit with understanding while magnifying God...this is the portal to Heaven. Our spirits are maintained in our earthly bodies but The Spirit gives us access to the portals of glory through our praise. Not getting it? Stephen was being stoned to death-heavy rocks hitting him and yet he looked and beheld the throne room of God! At the worst place in his physical life, he was immediately ushered into the best place of his life through praise! Y'all this....this is powerful! God, help us to see! Let us get our eyes off our circumstances and see you! Praise! Whatever you need to do to get there-get into the garment of praise...if that's putting a choir robe on or in your pajamas...if it's a walk outdoors or a closet inside...it's not really about the physical...it's about the mental...the place of worship. It's a choice not a circumstance. There's nothing God cannot do when we meet Him!

Steep in His words not man's words! Get your eyes on Him and away from the news media! Take off those outer garments of man's ways and slip into His promises...His words…

Distress that drives us to God does that. It turns us around. It gets us back in the way of salvation. We never regret that kind of pain. But those who let distress drive them away from God are full of regrets, end up on a deathbed of regrets.
2 Corinthians 7:10

Count It All Joy!

This is a picture of loss. This is my pup Bo, who has experienced the loss of his Suite mate Rudy, whom he has had with him his entire life and he has experienced a loss of freedom because the circumstances behind Rudy's demise make me more cautious with Bo. This is a picture of distress. You cannot hear the pitiful sounds coming from his whining that have distressed him so much that his cries keep the whole house awake as they are high pitched cries, even in sleeping. He is distressed at his loss of freedom because he makes poor choices when given that freedom.

Paul wrote to the Corinthians to count it all joy when trials came their way and to buck up when sorrows troubled them because we are not made of this world. He clipped their wings a bit and gave instructions to guide them which limited some freedoms and this distressed them. In this chapter Paul is upbeat because Titus has come to him and told him that the church at Corinth had used the "distress" they acquired through his previous letter to drive them closer to God.

As the keeper of Bo's freedoms and his authority right now, he follows me closely everywhere but he hasn't learned self control yet over his desires, so I cannot allow him his freedom. I know more than he does about this. He only has his eyes, nose & heart set on being free to do as he desires through the call of the wild nature in him. We are the same. We require guidance because we cannot see all the road in front of us nor know the lessons that must be trained into us, but God knows our situations and he has a plan that is perfect for us.

Regret is a hard pill to swallow especially when it leads to death. I regret letting Rudy roam free on Saturday. I may never know now what happened but I do know I had a choice and I chose incorrectly. I must live with those regrets. It's a hard pill to swallow. Regrets are something we all face because we all fight against the "leash" of God's boundaries. Our desires are human, natural and often hormonal. We are driven by the sin nature within us but God through His son's sacrifice made a way of atonement. He asked us to accept His gift of eternal life. His gift has strings attached. We must walk in the way He directs. He knows the path of freedom and fulfillment but He also sees the path to death and destruction. He knows the pitfalls and can see them ahead. He tightens the leash and redirects us through our problems and situations. Oh I can sense by now that you do not like the illustration of the leash. Why...is it because you feel demeaned by it? The truth is that we are bound by our sinful nature but that is a gilded cage skillfully woven for our demise much like a spider's web awaiting the prey. The leash on the other hand is so real...visible...obvious. I mean I prefer my own way, why would I choose to be directed by God's laws/instructions? It's a lesson of freedom to understand the protection of the Master's hand and to choose that protection over the call of sin nature. Being in the Master's way means He feeds me, clothes me, provides for me and directs my path. But does it mean I give up my perceived freedom to do what I want? Actually, no. God gives us more freedom than the gilded cage of sin. He allows us to see the pitfalls and choose the Master's direction or regret. He allows us to have freedom to choose His ways or the other. But there is always a choice. Don't be deceived into thinking there isn't. Choosing not to yield to God is choosing sides against Him. There is only one choice but it has the reward of eternity behind it. Yesterday Bo needed to be outside but he still was not in a place of good choices so I put him on a leading line that kept him in our yard. Oh this was so hard for him. I changed his circumstances to give him more freedom but his choices drove him to make himself more bound because he got wrapped up in trying to break free from the lead. Sometimes God gives us circumstances that drive us to our knees. This distress and not knowing of the path ahead causes us to fight what He has taught us. We fight against his promises. We fight against His leading. We fight against what we have learned of Him, and we end up more bound up because we refuse to just yield to His safekeeping. His ways aren't our ways but if we will learn and press into Him, the freedom is amazing. The places He takes us are beyond our wildest dreams. He is so faithful to His promises. Today, Lord, I choose to walk in your leadership. I choose to walk unencumbered by the weight of the world filled with distress and regret. I choose to breathe deeply in you and relax into your safekeeping for you know the path before me.

Where you lead I will follow.

11

But he's already made it plain
how to live, what to do,
what God is looking for in men
and women.
It's quite simple: Do what is
fair and just to your neighbor,
be compassionate and loyal in
your love,
And don't take yourself too
seriously—
take God seriously.

Micah 6: 8

The Joy Stealers!

"Life's not fair, get over it!" has been my saying of resiliency along with "No matter what life throws at you, He's still God". We have a lot of motivational sayings and speakers encouraging us to embrace "the secrets" of success and how to do things from marriage to raising kids. We have a lot of noise. It's the over complication of a simple concept that causes frustration, the most from basic math to complex marriage situations. So in Micah, the prophet, it is clarified. Don't take yourself seriously. Take God seriously. Don't get wrapped up in life's issues but rather let God handle it. Too many times we complicate things by overthinking them when if we would just rest in Him, His grace is enough. He said we are to treat others as we want to be treated: DO what is fair and just, love with compassion and mercy. BE compassionate and Loyal in love.
Fair doesn't mean equal. It means not to take advantage of...and "just" doesn't mean law but rather morally sound... So if we are to do what is right morally and not take advantage of others...these are concepts that deplete conflict which is the biggest joy stealer in our lives.
Conflict arises when there is an imbalance in standing between two people or things. When someone is having to make up the difference for someone else, the imbalance causes conflict. When life is out of balance in priorities, there is conflict. When your bones are out of balance, or your blood pressure or any of a number of other things in life, the imbalance causes physical conflict leading to inflammation and/or other issues. The point is that joy is not an emotion as much as it is a sense of balance achieved. The balance which is the key to JOY is in the alignment with God's principles.

If we DO what is fair and just then we have balance. Fair isn't equal. Fair is what is right. Think of all the problems that would be corrected if we correctly aligned to this. Too many times the word Fair is used to mean equity and a shifting of power balance is done under the guise of equality. So how do we make sure we are DOing what is right? Principle two, BE compassionate and loyal in love. Compassion is having concern for the welfare of others in unfortunate circumstances and Loyalty is firm and consistent in allegiance...so if we think of others first and do in love for them as Christ has done for us then the balance is restored. I've been doing PT (physical therapy) for months now even though I feel great most days. The PT is strengthening my muscle tone around my spine where I had surgery to maintain balance. When my muscles get out of balance, they pull on my bones making them out of alignment which causes pain. Think about it. The balance and alignment with God is our source of Joy! If we align ourselves in His keeping then we are filled from the source, but if we fail to do the work required to maintain alignment then the jostles of life pulling at us will take us out of alignment. Think of all the things that we do day to day which are not in alignment. When the balance shifts, we begin to be in pain in our relationships, our bodies, our minds, our spirits and we get to taking our situations so seriously that we lose Joy like a coffee cup pulled away from the stream of the pour. Then we are used up quickly, empty and exhausted. Alignment to God is like balancing and aligning the tires on our car. Sure, life brings things that cause us pain, flat tires, rough rides and sometimes even blowouts. But when we take ourselves to the Master Mechanic and request repair and alignment, He does all He needs to get us back in sync with Him. Then it is up to us to maintain alignment through reading His instructions (The Word) and applying the principles. Want joy? Check your alignment. The trip is much easier when the balance is restored.

With the arrival of Jesus, the Messiah, that fateful dilemma is resolved. Those who enter into Christ's being-here-for-us no longer have to live under a continuous, low-lying black cloud. A new power is in operation. The Spirit of life in Christ, like a strong wind, has magnificently cleared the air, freeing you from a fated lifetime of brutal tyranny at the hands of sin and death.

This resurrection life you received from God is not a timid, grave-tending life. It's adventurously expectant, greeting God with a childlike "What's next, Papa?" God's Spirit touches our spirits and confirms who we really are. We know who he is, and we know who we are: Father and children. And we know we are going to get what's coming to us—an unbelievable inheritance! We go through exactly what Christ goes through. If we go through the hard times with him, then we're certainly going to go through the good times with him!

Romans 8: 1-2, 15-17

Who's Your Papa?

I love the way my children can approach us naturally knowing that whatever they ask we will do to help them if it is in their best interest and within our power. God says he is just like this to us but even better because He knows what we think and are going to ask before we even ask and that if we ask in accordance with His plan in mind, anything we ask will be granted. Wow! That's an amazing God. "We have a great, big, wonderful God...The one who loves every one of us, is always watching over us, a great, big, wonderful God!" What would you do today if you knew that everything you asked would be granted and money was no object? Now think, is that according to the will of God? Let me give you a story. Wes and I had sold our house and not found another. We had packed everything up in anticipation of provision. We found a house and put a bid on it but it failed and I was feeling anxious. So I prayed and God impressed on me to go knock on a door to a house that I had seen a year earlier but was currently not for sale. I only had ten days until we were homeless and I was headed out of town for a corporate convention in just a few days. I knocked, they agreed to allow us a tour and we made an offer based on the sale of our other home. They accepted and even agreed to be out in ten days! That's a couple of miracles! Then as we got all things ready for a quick close (which is another miracle), on the day of closing, the bank called and said they had failed to do a paper for our loan so the VA had declined! We were homeless and I was bereft but I knew my God was my provider. I called upon him saying God, I know you own the cattle on a thousand hills. I need you to sell a few and provide a way for us according to your will. Minutes later, the President of the bank called me and said, since it was our mistake (miracle-bank admitting a mistake) we are going to finance your home loan in house (another miracle) and we are going to pay all closing costs (unbelievable, over the top, unexpected and unrequested Miracle)! You see, I had not asked God, but the home we were moving into had white carpet upstairs where my boys would be, and due to allergies, etc., this was not a good thing, so we had planned to save to replace the carpet, but God in His above-and-beyond way had seen my heart's desire and provided.

This is how miraculous it was. At closing, we received a cash check back for the exact amount to the penny that we would need to pay tithe and put wood floors upstairs. God did that! He went beyond what my expectations were. We can choose to walk in the belief of who He is or we can choose to walk in the weight of the oppression that our first world problems give us. I will tell you from experience that He is faithful. Never in my wildest dreams would I have seen this home as mine and yet it is because my Papa God decided He wanted to bless me. There is a simple freedom in the battlefield of life if you walk in His ways and His care. Are there troubles? You bet there are! But...and it's a big but...He is able to complete it, He is my weapon, my provider, my source, my healer, my all in all. He's my best friend, my help in trouble, my confidante and my confidence. He's my Papa! I love my biological daddy! I love him for all he is but I admire him most because he introduced me to Papa. God isn't a genie to jump to my whims but He is my provider in whom I can trust. The small things I worry about are nothing to His greatness. He wants us so much to keep our eyes on Him and not allow these earthly things to suppress us from experiencing His fullness. Are there highs/lows? Yes. Doubts and fears? Of course. Joys and triumphs? You bet.

Do things trouble us and make us question His goodness? Yes, we are human. He tells us that we all have trials and temptations but in every case he has made a way of escape for us. We must yield this life into His hands for safe keeping! If He chooses to take us forward into eternity...that is a gift, a blessing, and only a sorrow to those left behind. We must get our eyes off things of earth and look forward to the things He has. I promise you..,it's better than you imagine! Will you feel lonely and lost sometimes? Yes, it's that way in this world but He is a friend who sticks closer than a brother. Will you feel like God has failed you sometimes? Unfortunately, yes. Why? Because we look through the glass darkly. We turn on the light and cannot see beyond the mirror. God's ways aren't ours. We must accept that sometimes things will not go according to our plans but if we leave it to Him, He will work it out. As I've grown in Him, I have learned simple trust. Life isn't fair. Embrace Him and get over it. It's easy to get our eyes on things of earth and forget where we belong but we are king's kids and not just any king. He's the King of all Kings. No government can overshadow Him or outsmart Him. No authority can bypass Him. No person or being whether of The Heavens, Earth or below can outmaneuver Him. We are not limited to a timid, grave tending lifestyle. We are free. We have to embrace the freedom He has given us. His authority is ours. We must walk in it. We must be alive in Him. God's wind is blowing, clearing the air of the low hanging clouds of diseased defeat! He is getting our attention for something amazing before us. Quit focusing on the negative and get in line for the battlefields of glory. His weapons aren't made for flesh and blood...His weapons of warfare are much more powerful! Who He is...that's who created us, embedded us with His essence, His breath of life everlasting. That's who my Papa is. Who's your daddy?

And then God answered: "Write this.
Write what you see.
Write it out in big block letters
so that it can be read on the run.
This vision-message is a witness
pointing to what's coming.
It aches for the coming—it can hardly wait!
And it doesn't lie.
If it seems slow in coming, wait.
It's on its way. It will come right on time.

* * *

"Look at that man, bloated by self-importance—
full of himself but soul-empty.
But the person in right standing before God
through loyal and steady believing
is fully alive, really alive.

"But oh! God is in his holy Temple!
Quiet everyone—a holy silence. Listen!"

Habakkuk 2: 2-4, 20

Full of Self and Soul Empty!

Nature is a funny thing and the call of the wild is consuming. Recently our dogs heard the call due to a neighbor's dog being in heat. One of our dogs turned on the other and tore him up so he came limping home where we treated him and coddled him but he kept whining constantly so loud that my husband finally opened the garage and let him out. Where did he go? Right back to the place where he had just gotten hurt and this isn't the first time. My point is that the call of self-indulgence which is our sin nature is so strong that often we put ourselves back into situations that God has gotten us out of repeatedly because we have no self-control or discipline in our lives. I watched horrified as CA tried to pass a law to give animals the same rights as humans but in the same legislative session is considering a law to allow abortion or the murder of an innocent child until the moment of birth. Sin. Self-indulgence. But God, who has tolerated all of this for a time, is sending messages loud and clear to all letting them know enough is enough.

In Habakkuk 2, God tells the prophet to write the message large and on the walls so people can see while going about their business, like on a billboard. He calls out to His people telling them it will not be long and not to get weary in the waiting because he sees the self-indulged and their acts...and they are soul empty living only for more and more wealth, sacrificing others and the eternal for the mortal which will not last. He cautions us to be aware of God in His temple-a Holy Silence. Know this that we are His Holy Temple. We are His dwelling place. We are who He is calling to walk calmly before Him.

When you read the full chapter, you will see it is a calling out of the wicked to the judgment that is coming for them. You can pick up a verse and see how it describes people in our government and society now, who are so self absorbed that they lead everyone into sin and care nothing for anyone except themselves, but they are an empty shell. Fully alive! That is how the person walking before God humbly and devotedly is described. It doesn't matter what the outer shell is, life comes from the inside. When you witness success, you have a pull to do what that person does. When you witness life alive, you see the draw. Success doesn't come from self-indulgence nor from wealth nor from a quick formula nor a perception of knowing. True Success is God given life inside. Pushing to accomplish life here isn't what God has called us to do/be. Yes, He says "whatsoever your hand finds to do, do with all your heart, soul, mind and strength according to the Lord" meaning to do those things that are pleasing to God with all of you.

I don't do things in halves but rather with all of me. When people look at me, they see different things but what I want them to see is God's love. I want them to see Jesus in Me. I want to be a walking billboard of His faithfulness and His love. So here's the question: what is written on my walking billboard of life for others to read: From my FB to my actions? Do they read self-indulgence or self-sacrifice? Do they read worldly wealth or Heavenly wealth? Are they reading words of wisdom falling from the throne of grace or a quick fix solution of self-indulgence? What is my billboard of life advertising? Do they see Jesus in Me?

Lord, let my life be about healing broken people. Please use me. If my billboard has gotten distorted, I ask that you clear it to read only what you have to say. Let me walk in your power and might so that others are drawn to you. Help me to be humble, patient and willing to wait for your glory and not feel the call of man's success so that I sacrifice a moment with you. "Is the face that I see in the mirror, the one I want others to see?" Is it you or is it me? Help me Lord to be a reflection only of you and not overshadowed by my own self-importance. Use me. Let me be quiet in your Holy Temple so that you God can shine through me. "Love through me. Let my hands reach out to others. There's a lonely person somewhere needing just one friend to care-touch through me Holy Spirit-love through me."

God is good,
a hiding place in tough times.
He recognizes and welcomes
anyone looking for help,
No matter how desperate the trouble.
But cozy islands of escape
He wipes right off the map.
No one gets away from God.
Why waste time conniving against God?
He's putting an end to all such scheming.
For troublemakers, no second chances.
Like a pile of dry brush,
Soaked in oil,
they'll go up in flames.

Nahum 1; 7-10

The Cozy Flame!

I've always loved a nice fire when it is controlled by the fireplace or fire pit but a burning brush fire makes me nervous, unless Wes is close, because I know he'll do his best to control it. God is still a pillar of fire but one that is controlled by His own boundaries. Fire is a multifaceted thing. It's helpful and harmful depending on how it is used and God himself also is multifaceted. I think of how God spoke to Moses from an unconsumed burning bush foreshadowing the pillar of fire that would guide the Israelites. In Nahum, we often quote the verse about God being our hiding place and our source of refuge but he's so much more! God is our source but He is also our protector and judge. Today my heart thinks of all the cries of the innocent who have been slaughtered in the womb and how they cried out in pain. God heard every cry and He is not deaf to their suffering. He took them to Heaven to be with Him and their blood will be revenged on those who continually push this evil agenda of death. This God is not a welcome comfort of fire but rather a flame headed towards those who are dry kindling having soaked themselves in the kerosene of innocent blood. They cannot escape to their islands of refuge for God knows where they are. Epstein thought he had it all and he is now burning alive, never consumed, in hell.

That is the destination of all who become dry kindling by first not abiding in the vine.

Yesterday I took a lot of mint leaves off my plant, chopped them up and put them on a pan in the sun to dry out. Very quickly in that heat, they became brittle and crumbled into nothingness which I then used to make fragrant tea. Sometimes we feel like we are plucked from the vine and crushed up, consumed by the world but the Master still uses us to bring fragrance as His water of life pours through us. I think of Samson. He chose to leave the vine and quickly was crushed and used by the world but He remembered His maker and cried out. God heard Him and despite his willful rejection of God, the fire once more fell on him allowing Him to be used up for God's purposes. Do you know how mighty he was when he was used by God? His story is phenomenal but he chose the world and outside the fire of protection the flames consumed him until he was dry kindling. The difference is that He chose for God to wash him once again in anointing oil rather than the kerosene of the world. And in that moment when God's flame touched him again, he was consumed with purpose. How can I live in the place where God wants me? Stay in The Vine where the living water constantly flows through you, using you for His purposes. What if I have become dry kindling used up by the world soaked in the kerosene of sin? There is still time for repentance where the precious blood of Christ and His anointing can cover you and use you for His glory! Fire. The symbol of the power of God's might will consume all in its path in the end days. You can be a bush covered in Jesus' blood plugged into the Vine with roots in the living water that remains unconsumed. Or you can dwell in the places of wickedness, as dry kindling soaking in the kerosene of the world's ways, awaiting the All Consuming Fire to send you to hell to burn for eternity. God created us in His image as eternal beings with ethereal bodies that inhabit this place for a period of time in a corporeal body. This corporeal body is not your purpose nor your end. Once you embrace that and begin to see your true purpose in Him, you will realize the truth and it will set you free. Our minds are finite and it is easy to get caught up in the here and now. But the God of All is calling you to hear His voice from the pillar of Fire by night. He is urging you to draw near to Him for His flame of anger is burning hot towards those who have rejected and despised His son, Jesus. What will the pillar of fire be to you: A place of refuge and safety or a raging inferno consuming you as dry kindling whetted in the kerosene of appetites of the world? It is your choice and mine. Lord, I want to be used by you; a burning bush of your purpose, unconsumed and devoted to your purpose. It is my desire to live for Jesus.

19

"These words I speak to you are not incidental additions to your life, homeowner improvements to your standard of living. They are foundational words, words to build a life on. If you work these words into your life, you are like a smart carpenter who built his house on solid rock. Rain poured down, the river flooded, a tornado hit—but nothing moved that house. It was fixed to the rock. "But if you just use my words in Bible studies and don't work them into your life, you are like a stupid carpenter who built his house on the sandy beach. When a storm rolled in and the waves came up, it collapsed like a house of cards."

Matthew 7: 24-27

A Solid Foundation!

Watched a video yesterday of people repairing their walls and even sinks/toilets with Ramen noodles. It cracked me up! First, you eat something that can repair walls and toilets? Second, you want a shortcut so bad you use noodles to repair? Do you think that's going to last? Like really? Shortcuts. Everyone wants the easy quick fix. I hear it every day. People who grab meds to treat attention issues rather than train them. People who choose meds to diet/exercise...I may be guilty of trying something like this once or twice...in my life but the shortcut never works out.

Life is hard work. Relationships are hard work. Jesus who was raised in a carpenter's home uses this scripture picture of building a house to illustrate for us in Matthew 7 the concepts of making the right choice and doing the hard work.
A life foundation of God's word is strong and can withstand the tornadoes of life but a house built on quick quirky sayings pulled in pieces from the word is like building with Ramen noodles. It may pass the look test, but it won't pass the longevity test.

Jesus tells us to build our home's foundation in Him. This doesn't mean you go around writing scripture on the concrete and wood, although I have seen people do that symbolically as they pray over their home and I think God honors that too. What it actually means is that you rock into your life The Word. His words become your breath, and your life is based on this solidness because this world will rock you to your core. The stock market isn't the answer, buying up investments in gold/silver/land/oil isn't the answer. Knowing who He is...that's the answer. It's foundation. Wes built a table out of these huge beams from an old house he tore down. That table is rock solid and going nowhere anytime soon...would take many men to move it...because it has a strong foundation. Foundations aren't just concrete, rock and wood. But Christ Jesus is our solid rock. He is our source. Our help in time of trouble. He is strong enough and certain enough for any storm. I know so many going through hard places and things right now. I want to encourage you to hang on because although the ride may get rough,
"Our hope is built on nothing less than Jesus' blood and righteousness."

"I am the Real Vine and my Father is the Farmer. He cuts off every branch of me that doesn't bear grapes. And every branch that is grape-bearing he prunes back so it will bear even more. You are already pruned back by the message I have spoken.

"Live in me. Make your home in me just as I do in you. In the same way that a branch can't bear grapes by itself but only by being joined to the vine, you can't bear fruit unless you are joined with me.

"You didn't choose me, remember; I chose you, and put you in the world to bear fruit, fruit that won't spoil. As fruit bearers, whatever you ask the Father in relation to me, he gives you. "But remember the root command: Love one another.

Jhon 15: 1-4, 16-17

He Chose Me!

The seeds took root and began to grow, not looking like much more than a weed. Then the farmer had to choose which to pull. You see there are only so many that can go the mile and produce the necessary crop. If I were the farmer, I'd let them all try to make it which as I've been told would result in overcrowded fields, not enough nutrients and a poor crop. But the farmer has to choose which to pull and which to prune back all through the growth process. I've always read John 15 with the knowledge that God is the farmer and He makes the choices which are sometimes not popular. He takes some home early to be with Him, which is hard for us to see and endure. Some of our crops get diseases and other pests, which shortens our life span, and the farmer again pulls that crop up to take it early.

The crop he chooses continues to grow and be pruned through the storms and hot weather. Sometimes the weather beats down so hard that the crop leans over and droops but soon the "Son" will shine again on them and they will once again blossom in the love/joy of the Savior. The last scripture in John 15 is Jesus telling us that He chose us. And that whatever we ask in His name be-lieving in faith, His father will answer...then He says pay attention to the root command...the root command in anything is the on/off, the kill switch, the core. The root command He gives...love one another. Wow! So when I ask anything of God, it must have the root command examined. Was it asked in love for others? That's powerful and tough. He chose me to walk in His Sonlight reflecting His love on others. He chose me to bear fruit so that others may be fed on His life, love, kindness by the fruit of joy, peace, patience, self-control. He chose me to bear this disease, problem, etc. so that I, walking in Him, can demonstrate to others how to live in His reflection not my own. He chose me to follow Him. That means not looking back on the could've beens but looking forward to his purpose. He chose me to wear His authority but all I do must be rooted in love.

When I begin to grow into areas He doesn't see benefits in for His purposes, I will be pruned. Sometimes when I do everything right, I still get pruned because that keeps me healthy and able to produce more. It's hard to see that the things we go through from the worst to the best are tools of growth but that's what they are. Sunflowers are grown as a crop. They may be pretty to look at and magnificent in their majesty but they are grown for their seed and their oil. They ultimately will be sacrificed for the crop just as we ultimately will give all for His love. Chosen. What a great place to be! Lord, help me to remember when I am walking in hardship that you chose me. Help me to hold my head up high and reflect your love through my hard times and my good times. Let me be the reflection you want me to be of your glory and help me to stay rooted in your love. Chosen. Root command; love one another.

"In prayer there is a connection between what God does and what you do. You can't get forgiveness from God, for instance, without also forgiving others. If you refuse to do your part, you cut yourself off from God's part.

"Give your entire attention to what God is doing right now, and don't get worked up about what may or may not happen tomorrow. God will help you deal with whatever hard things come up when the time comes.

Matthew 6: 14-15, 34

Making the Deal!

Recently I made a deal with someone who did not hold up their part of the bargain. Not because they couldn't but simply because they were not truly invested in the outcome. When you are working towards a goal and only one person in the group is doing all the work, resentment begins to build up and cause angst. Most of us try this same "bargaining" with God and often get disappointed because we feel like we have done our part and He has not, which is what Jesus is speaking about here in these verses in Matthew. He is speaking about our prayer relationship with God and discussing how it isn't about the show of "God Can versus God Will". It's not about whether He can or will move in a situation but rather about our right standing. You see often the perception of doing our part while the other fails to do theirs is perceived. Last year, my son had a group project and the group would not give him anything to do...these girls wanted to make sure it was done right in their eyes, so they did it their way, then submitted it saying he had done nothing. While true, he was blocked from doing anything because they refused to allow him to do his part. This is the way we often are with God. We pray about it and say God I need you to do...but then in our rush/hurry/control needs, we do it all and miss out on God's blessings. So many times we see this in scripture where the lack of faith or lack of waiting got the people into situations, from Abraham & Sarah trying to make God's promise happen in the natural instead of the supernatural, resulting in Ishmael not being of God's promise, but rather of man's deeds, to Esau selling the birthright for porridge because he didn't value it as God's promise but rather man's math of 50/50.

Making a deal with God isn't walking in His promises. Jesus said that in prayer there is a connection between us and God. He said if you refuse to do your part in the work of God in your life then He cannot do His. If you don't turn the project over to Him, His part will not be done. If you don't allow Him to do the work in you to prepare you for what He has, His part cannot be fulfilled. Jesus' direction to us was to give our ENTIRE attention to what God is doing right now and to stop worrying/fretting about the next step. This is our part. We are to pray, ask, work to align ourselves in the way He instructs and then rest in His promises. Be still and know He is God. I know this is hard. Believe me. I'm not a still person. I get distracted easily by the things happening around me. When we are training attention at my office, we load to get the brain overwhelmed then unload to allow the brain to process more effectively. Sometimes I see God doing this in my life. He gives me much more than I can handle so I feel overwhelmed then He takes those burdens as I ask, allowing me to rest in him. But, I must give them to Him or I continue carrying more than He ever intended for me.

The weight's got you down, give it over to Jesus and start looking at the road in front of you as a beautiful place of freedom relying on Him. Getting overwhelmed, give it over to Him to do His part. Feeling discouraged or disappointed in God, tell Him about it and then work on your faith. Begin to look around and count your blessings knowing that He has all things set before you that are good. Trust. This is the connection in prayer. Trust isn't knowing God can but knowing God will. Faith is the substance of things hoped for and the evidence of things not seen. Faith isn't faith until it is all you're holding onto. When the project is in His hands and you are trusting Him to complete it, turn it in and reap the rewards, then you've done your part.
Step up and step out in faith.

Many words rush along like rivers in flood,
but deep wisdom flows up from artesian
springs.

Answering before listening
is both stupid and rude.

Wise men and women are always learning,
always listening for fresh insights.

Words satisfy the mind as much as fruit does the
stomach;good talk is as gratifying as a good
harvest. Words kill, words give life;
they're either poison or fruit—you choose.

Provebs 18: 4, 13, 15, 20-21

Wonderful Words of Life!

There is nothing as beautiful as a deep stream or flow of living water. My friend Susan took this picture at Horseshoe Canyon in the Rio Grande Valley area and you can see the beauty of the natural spring feeding the stream of water. It's refreshed constantly by the source. I'm a talker and a listener which is sorta a rare combination because it's hard to do one when you are the other. I prefer to be a listener. I love the flow of conversation and the ambience of words. I'm fascinated with how God used man to write His words intricately for our instruction manual. The value of words and the ability to speak life through them is phenomenal and unlike anything else...this ability created our world. In the beginning of the world, God spoke and His words created from nothingness. Wow! Hold on! Think of that! Listen for a minute! He said "Let there be..." and it was! Miracle after miracle occurred in scripture...most of them became because of words spoken and actions followed. Jesus said Lazarus come forth and he did! But when The Word Himself lay in a tomb...not a word was spoken... until after He rose! God uses the power of words to change lives. He uses the power in our words to bring life but they can also bring death. Words lie in the power of the tongue and very often now in the power of the pen or the fingers on a keyboard. Words...speaking...listening...hearing…sharing...believing...the power of the word is in the embrace. A word spoken in anger can tear another down or ruin a marriage. A word spoken in fear can cause entire economies to collapse.

A word spoken in faith can move mountains, cause the dead to rise and remove cancer. A word with the right ingredients around it has power but The Word has all power. Your words can be driven by the source of The Word or they can be driven by selfish ambition. The challenge is in the source. Lots of talk out there about disinformation and releasing addresses and people's opinions on so many things. Words strung together can become a beautiful song that brings joy and emotion or in a poem to bring sweet memories or in a book to teach others or take them on a journey. I love words...they are part of my love language. Words of affirmation bring me my greatest accolades but also hurt me deeply when used as a battering ram. But these words only have the power that I give them. The power of the words is given by the giver and the receiver of those words. You have a choice to receive the words and allow them to speak into your life or not to have value in your life. Words have power given to them but you must choose. As I sit here contemplating my day, I want to embrace The Word of Life! God's words speak life. I choose The Words of Life not the spoken/texted/typed words of death. I choose to embrace words that uplift and words that breathe life. Lord, today let my words heal a heart that hurts. Let my words be balm to a soul and be used by you to bring life.

Lord, I ask that you infuse your words of life into my very being so that as I go forth, I bring life to those around me. Let me be your words extended. Let Your Sonlight reflect through my words into the lives of others. Beautiful words, wonderful words...of Life!

"Count on it: Everyone who had it in for you
will end up out in the cold—
real losers.
Those who worked against you
will end up empty-handed—
nothing to show for their lives.
When you go out looking for your old
adversaries
you won't find them—
Not a trace of your old enemies,
not even a memory.
That's right. Because I, your God,
have a firm grip on you and I'm not letting go.
I'm telling you, 'Don't panic.
I'm right here to help you.'

Isaiah 41: 11-13

Sheltered In The Arms of God!

God says I have a firm grip on you and I'm not letting go. Most days don't go like I expect them to go. There are ups and downs but the constant is His presence. There's nothing quite like a hug of safety. A hug that holds you until you let go. If you are reading this, imagine a hug-arms of safety and strength wrapped around you. This is what sheltering is. Sheltered by God is a place of protection in times of trouble or refuge from storms. Sheltered by God is also a hug in the good times. Sheltered by God is a constant. He is there in the good and the bad. The Israelites walked in the shelter of God Almighty as a pillar of cloud by day and a pillar of fire by night. I cannot help but imagine the complete peace that it would bring just knowing that you could see evidence of God's presence constantly, but wait...we can. Nature around us has highs and lows but is constantly singing of His presence. When God created all things, he gave all things a voice, a communication unique to Him and that creation. God said if we don't worship Him, the rocks will cry out. I love the song, "When God Ran" because I can just see God moving in my direction to provide shelter when I had turned from Him, but yet He was there. In Exodus it says the cloud did not depart from them. Scholars have a timeline and discuss Joshua's crossing into Jericho across the Jordan as the time when the Israelites no longer saw the pillar of cloud/fire visibly, but long before that occurred the people failed God. In fact, with all the miracles and wonders, with visible evidence of God in front of them...they still walked away from His provision and His shelter. They grumbled, complained, and screamed in anger. The moment the cloud lifted into the mountain as Moses met with God, the people betrayed God for false idols they built. This is exactly how we are today. We struggle and whine, complain and throw fits like toddlers in the presence of a tolerant parent.

Then the moment that God seems to not be watching and tuned into us, we look around for another source. The God of Miracles is still present in our midst. The cloud that provided cover is still there... He's not departed. He's still our fire by night providing warmth and light in our darkest situations. He's still our shelter from the sun and a cool place to collect ourselves in our weaknesses. You see the Israelites like us turned their back to the pillar as they went about their daily tasks. They forgot His presence and all they had to do was turn to see. We are more blessed. We just have to make a heart turn and He runs to us, takes us in His arms again to shelter us. What will it take for you? When will you realize His love and reach out for His arms of love? He's waiting with open arms, running in your direction...His grace is enough.

Knowing what is right is like deep water in the heart; a wise person draws from the well within.

Drinking from the beautiful chalice of knowledge is better than adorning oneself with gold and rare gems.

The very steps we take come from God; otherwise how would we know where we're going?

God is in charge of human life, watching and examining us inside and out.

Proverbs 20: 5, 15, 24, 27

The Knowing!

I am not one who knows everything but I do love to learn and share what I have learned. I love to read. I used to read a book a night and hope to get back there as my neck/back tolerates it. But there is a deeper knowing that is even better than knowledge. It's a God confidence. Self-esteem is a minefield as there is a fine line between humbleness and pride. I cannot tell you how much I love seeing the lifting of heads when a client who was beat down by inability becomes able to learn easily. Their whole demeanor lifts. They become proud of themselves and what they can do. I love seeing that and I love seeing those that recognize their cognitive trainer as the person who helped them up. When we set a training plan in place, it is a blueprint but the trainer takes that blueprint and guides the process by refining those skills through intensive therapy. The client must be willing to put in the hard work and challenges must be met in order to accomplish the goals. God orders our steps. He has a blueprint for our lives and He gave us His word as a guide but we must be willing to put in the time/efforts needed to develop the skills He wants us to have. It's training. The cognitive trainer learns the students tendencies and motivations while they work together so they can push them to efficiency and automaticity. When you first learn to do anything, you aren't extremely great at it but drilling and practicing it helps you refine it.

God's deep well of knowing would drown us if He were to pour all into us immediately. Instead He allows us to draw on His wealth of knowing as needed but it requires us to know the process to become efficient at it. In Psalms, David says the sheep know His voice because David was a shepherd but a generation later, Solomon, who is David's son, says it here in Proverbs as drawing from the deep water in the heart and drinking from a beautiful cup because Solomon had only known riches and authority as a king's kid. He was given the gift of wisdom along with wealth because when God asked him what he wanted, he asked for wisdom not wealth.The crux of this is understanding that God is in control and provides us source and resources as needed but to automatically draw from them we must know them. A rich man who has earned his way is well versed in money and automation of using it. A skilled carpenter knows his tools and his trade. A trained athlete knows his craft and automatically performs what he has practiced over and over.

By training in the knowledge of God's word, we automatically learn the right. Knowing what is right automatically is a deep well of infinite source. It is water on demand straight to the cup to be drunk. Tapping into the source, knowing His words inside and out, hearing his voice and knowing it is Him takes practice. We must learn by putting ourselves into the word daily, habitually, so that it is our source and we can automatically draw on it without thinking in our time of need.

As a cognitive trainer, it is my job to train brains to function automatically and efficiently. We practice the memory skills over and over to develop motor memory of use. We train the brain to pay attention by distraction. We train the processing speed by moving things faster and faster. All this is done so that when the client leaves us, the skills are theirs to use automatically whenever they need them.

God has us in training too! He is our source trainer. He gave us work to do to progress our skills so that in time of need, we can automatically draw on our knowledge of Him. It's time to put in the hard work so the automaticity of trusting/ knowing is there when it is needed.

Where do you think all these appalling wars and quarrels come from? Do you think they just happen? Think again. They come about because you want your own way, and fight for it deep inside yourselves. You lust for what you don't have and are willing to kill to get it. You want what isn't yours and will risk violence to get your hands on it. You wouldn't think of just asking God for it, would you? And why not? Because you know you'd be asking for what you have no right to. You're spoiled children, each wanting your own way. You're cheating on God. If all you want is your own way, flirting with the world every chance you get, you end up enemies of God and his way. And do you suppose God doesn't care? The proverb has it that "he's a fiercely jealous lover." And what he gives in love is far better than anything else you'll find. It's common knowledge that "God goes against the willful proud; God gives grace to the willing humble."

As it is, you are full of your grandiose selves. All such vaunting self-importance is evil. In fact, if you know the right thing to do and don't do it, that, for you, is evil.

James 4: 2-6, 16-17

The Good, The Proud and The Humble!

Yesterday, I taught children's church and in kids there is no guile. They don't pretend. They just are. We had an obstacle course with rules to go through and the best time won. Kids reflect us. They are like a mini community and of course there was pride, cheering, cheating and jeering. The nature of man not God took hold in most kids. This is the battle not the race itself. These kids were doing what is our sin nature to do...fight to win no matter what...be the top dog even if it hurts others or requires cheating...the natural order....but that is not God's way. In this lesson it was purposeful because it allowed the lesson of Ministry and self sacrifice to be taught. The winner was awarded the prize but not the praise until after we discussed our human nature which is to wow at the fall but fail to acknowledge the wins. When obstacles get in our way, we tend to fight tooth and nail for ourselves against others.

The truth is we need a helping hand to get us through. Then we saw it...God's love in action as a little one struggled...the task looked impossible to her and she began to cry but someone stepped up to her and gave her his hand...just like God does to us when we on this obstacle course of life begin to cry out, God steps in and gives us a hand. She wasn't the winner in this scenario but she completed the course and had cheers from the other kids which is all she needed. She had accomplished the purpose with help and she was content. This is how love plays in our life.

Human nature wants its own way. It wants to win and deep inside we fight for it. It is so hard to do what is right when it is against our natural man. But God says in His word that to know to do right and to choose not to do so is sin and evil. Our world is fraught with the dog eat dog mentality. I just experienced that literally as my dogs fought over a female that was in heat. Rudy tore Bo up and Bo came limping home as Rudy went back to following the female ignoring our rules and following his nature. That was the last time we saw him. Unfortunately that desire to win over all others took his life against bigger dogs and wild animals. We tried to get him to return home just as we tried keeping him in our home but his wild nature took precedence. This is where all the wars and battles come in...sin nature must have its own way crushing others in its path but God's way is love. So if our sin nature is so strong, how do we live a life reflecting God's love? Stay plugged in. Keep listening for His voice. See others through His eyes not your own. Reach out in His love and not your own abilities. His strength is perfect. When you cannot go on, reach to Him...He's right there. We are flesh and our sin nature is demanding but God indwells in those of us who have chosen to follow Him.
We are not perfect but we are His.

Lean into His ways and don't demand your own. His strength is enough. Do your best, trust Him for the rest. Our kids at our church are pretty amazing because they get it. As we ended our day with a mission in our minds, I watched their demeanors change towards one another. They leaned into God's way and the whole atmosphere shifted. That is how people know we are His...The fragrance of His love changes the atmosphere. Press into His nature today instead of your own and watch doors open.

Use your heads as you live and work among outsiders. Don't miss a trick. Make the most of every opportunity. Be gracious in your speech. The goal is to bring out the best in others in a conversation, not put them down, not cut them out.

Colossians 4: 5-6

Putting Out Your Best!

Wes' grandma gave us some china when we first married that we have used only once in 25 years. Mostly because we don't entertain much and boys with paper plates is a much better idea when their favorite past-time is flying plates. The best we had was not a consideration and now...the plates have sat unused for 25 years. What is it about us that reserves the best for a day that never comes, failing to realize that time has passed and the best reality has happened while you were waiting? I'm a words of affirmation girl so the adage of sticks and stones isn't true in my life at all. Words hurt me or heal me but I withdraw from people who don't use their words wisely. Words have power and using them negatively to beat someone up is just as powerful as using your fists even though the government may not recognize it as much, as far as punishment. Words have power to life, security and peace. They can bring up or tear down. We are instructed here to use our speech graciously to lift others up and bring out the good. A kind word is like honey on lips the psalmist says. In my career I have learned that words have power long past the use of them and words carelessly said may write on someone's life more than you think. Scripture tells us there is power in the tongue to give life or kill. Words have killed marriages, relationships, careers, and countries. Our words are a resource to be used in His love and in giving life to others. Guard your tongue. Be wise. A word said in haste or frustration can tear someone down. A word given in love can restore the broken. How are you using your words? Father, help me, Lord, to be conscientious of my words and deeds. I ask you to stop me from saying anything that would tear another down. Allow my words to bring love, peace and joy to others so I may be a reflection of you for your glory.

Today is the day for your best...use your best words, your best china and the best of all God has given you to bless another.

For an answer Jesus called over a child, whom he stood in the middle of the room, and said, "I'm telling you, once and for all, that unless you return to square one and start over like children, you're not even going to get a look at the kingdom, let alone get in. Whoever becomes simple and elemental again, like this child, will rank high in God's kingdom. What's more, when you receive the childlike on my account, it's the same as receiving me.

"Watch that you don't treat a single one of these childlike believers arrogantly. You realize, don't you, that their personal angels are constantly in touch with my Father in heaven?

Matthew 18: 2-5, 10

It's Elementary My Dear...!

My heart sank when I heard of another school shooting especially as this one was at my elementary school. I was an "other" at school because I lived close to the border and was one of the only English speaking children attending school in Uvalde in those days. The simplicity of our experiences and expectations from that time is something I see in many of the little ones I work with at LearningRx. It's a pure belief that people are basically good and out to help, but sometimes this isn't accurate with people. Sometimes their simple childlike approach to life has lost its joy and has become more than they can bear, so evil strikes out as it is the man they have fed. We are born into a sin nature with our angelic soul immediately at war and the being that is fed in our life grows stronger. This is why Matthew records this interaction of Jesus with His children and His words. A child is born with a simple, uncomplicated tendency to trust as they have not had their trust which is God instilled stolen from them. I have several friends who work neonatal intensive care. They tell me that these babies born so early with so many issues still recognize their mother's voice and still trust, despite all the pain/procedures they go through. Yes, that self nature to satisfy hunger, safety and rest are there but so is trust. A childlike faith is a well of trust.

There isn't a much harder thing to watch than someone who begins losing their memory and starting back down with dementia. But the thing is as that person fades...the selfishness gets lost and the childlike nature of trust is there...

The simple childlike faith is the key...it's the element that unlocks the power of God's love and activates His heart actions. He loves us so. Oh How He loves you and me. Such a simple thing with huge rewards. I have a prize cabinet at my office and kids see the rewards and immediately want...they work hard in their sessions to earn points toward the prizes. The points are saved towards a goal much like we are laying up treasures above where nothing can steal or ruin it. Our eternal reward is the Blessed Hope. The childlike mind lets go of the need to be held to this world. As Dr Watson was told often by Sherlock Holmes, it's elementary my dear...such a simple thing...
trust in God through all things and treat others with His love.

Let go and Let God.

Thomas said, "Master, we have no idea where you're going. How do you expect us to know the road?"

Jesus said, "I am the Road, also the Truth, also the Life. No one gets to the Father apart from me. If you really knew me, you would know my Father as well. From now on, you do know him. You've even seen him!"

"You've been with me all this time, Philip, and you still don't understand? To see me is to see the Father. So how can you ask, 'Where is the Father?' Don't you believe that I am in the Father and the Father is in me? The words that I speak to you aren't mere words. I don't just make them up on my own. The Father who resides in me crafts each word into a divine act.

John 14: 5-7, 9-10

GPS (God Positioning System)!

I must admit I'm a little like Thomas sometimes...getting led easily in the misdirections of life. So easy to think you have it all together then wham! Life hits. Jesus said each word spoken in His name is a divine act. Wait...what? Seriously? The words I speak have that much power? Absolutely. As a brain trainer, we train our clients to understand the power of mindset. A growth mindset allows for possibilities that are endless. It says, I don't know it all YET... but I am willing to learn. I think this is what Jesus is telling Thomas here. Wow, dude, you've been walking/talking/experiencing God in your presence for like how many years and you still don't get it when tough times come? Thomas is like, well, I've been following you and not really watching the road so I don't know where to go from here. Jesus again...you have been watching the road because I am the road...I am the way, the truth, the life. All you gotta do is trust me and I'll guide you. Thomas-yeah, that's kinda my issue...I have trust issues...I mean, I know you say you are God and I've seen and experienced lots of miracles from healing the blind and lepers to raising the dead and I've watched you move time and again in situations of provision, from gold from a fish's mouth to turning a loaf of bread into a feast, but still...I just have like these major trust issues. Jesus-seriously, man? You have touched me, felt my presence, experienced all these things and you still doubt me? Good thing my words don't depend on your belief!! My Father God crafts every word I say into a divine act!

This is my translation of that talk because like I said, Jesus & I have had this conversation and not just once. I am so grateful that He is so patient with me. He's a friend like no other. He gets it when no one else does. He sees more than you say and He feels every breath, heartbeat, sorrow. He understands on a deeper level and He's real. So yes, my conversations with God/Jesus/Holy Spirit are just like this. He gets me. My GPS is Him. He's my way, my truth, my light, my life...He's my God Positioning System and he corrects me-reroutes me, when I get all turned around.

Grace...the GPS I rely on!

Later on that day, the disciples had
gathered together, but, fearful of the Jews, had
locked all the doors in the house. Jesus
entered, stood among them, and said, "Peace to you."
Then he showed them his hands and side.
The disciples, seeing the Master with their own eyes,
were awestruck. Jesus repeated his greeting: "Peace
to you. Just as the
Father sent me, I send you."

Jesus said, "So, you believe because you've seen
with your own eyes. Even better blessings are in
store for those who believe without seeing."
Jesus provided far more God-revealing signs than are
written down in this book. These are written down so
you will believe that Jesus is the Messiah, the Son of
God, and in the act of believing, have real and eternal
life in the way he personally revealed it.

John 20: 20-21, 29-31

God of Hope Who Conquers Fear!

Lord, I believe but help my unbelief. These are the words of a parent who had just been told by Jesus that his son who struggled with demon possession could be healed. Fear...the factor that paralyzes us or changes us into our most base self...fear..brings fight or flight...for most it is flight. If you don't believe that, look around. In country after country, people who live in fear turn towards hope...they flee their current circumstances and run towards hope. The disciples were no different. They betrayed, denied and deserted Jesus and were hiding in fear for their lives when Jesus appeared.

Fear is overwhelming and earth shaking...it drives policies, political decisions and is created by people for this purpose because it is a motivation. Hope is also a driver and a motivator. In this passage, John is telling us that fear without hope brings death just like works without faith. The people who walked and talked with Jesus lost faith and huddled in fear until he reappeared and reignited their hope...I want you to read this chapter...because after he tells them, proves to them who He is...He actually breathes new life into the room...He breathed out the Holy Spirit to infill them, but though they carried the breath of God within them...it wasn't activated until they went through a period of anxiety, waiting and prayer to conquer it. I wish you could be here right now and see/feel His Spirit moving...

My champion is not dead...He is alive. The lover of our souls isn't just a man who passed through earth leaving promises but The God of all creation, who took on the form of mortal man humbly knowing He would suffer a horrendous death on a cross and have to physically go into the grave to conquer death once and for all.

We mourn because we do not understand. We mourn because our brains and hearts cannot grasp the eternal. We mourn because the things we put stock into fail. We mourn because our eyes and our hopes are placed wrongly. Jesus tells us to get our eyes off things of earth and begin to focus on His vision...His ways...His purpose and He will activate the Spirit He has breathed into us. It requires walking into a new dimension of belief. It requires laying aside the hopes/dreams of mankind, limited by the laws of man, to embrace the Eternal Hope and walk in the cloud of miracles.

I like to walk each morning and many mornings as I walk, I feel the clouds around me as I walk, as a cool blanket of mist...think of it. We walk in the cloud of His presence when we spend time taking Him in.
Are we walking in the cloud of miracles and failing to do what it takes to activate them in our lives and the lives of others? Are we walking in inactivated faith because we are allowing doubt/fear to cloud our minds? Are we simply going passively through the motions of life never realizing that our faith must arise to activate the Eternal Hope?
Jesus is coming back whether we are ready or not.

Wes' garden will grow whether he does anything more to it at all, but if he doesn't care for it, hope for it and work on it...it will not produce at the level it could...just think...we are walking in a cloud of miracles...Lord, I believe...help my unbelief. I choose to trust you!

Lean into His Hope. Get your eyes off the things of Earth and focus on Him. Then you can truly see what reality is...a place of faith or fear...a place of Hope or Despair....a place of belief or discouragement. Your choice...see through your eyes or His...Lord, I trust in you. Your vision is better than mine. Your purposes and plans far exceed my expectations. Lord I believe but help my unbelief.

If I give everything I own to the poor and even go to the stake to be burned as a martyr, but I don't love, I've gotten nowhere. So, no matter what I say, what I believe, and what I do, I'm bankrupt without love.
Love never gives up.
Love cares more for others than for self.
Love doesn't want what it doesn't have.
Love doesn't strut,
Doesn't have a swelled head,
Doesn't force itself on others,
Isn't always "me first,"
Doesn't fly off the handle,
Doesn't keep score of the sins of others,
Doesn't revel when others grovel,
Takes pleasure in the flowering of truth,
Puts up with anything,
Trusts God always,
Always looks for the best,
Never looks back,
But keeps going to the end.

1 Corinthians 13: 3-7

Bankrupt Without Love!

1 Corinthians 13 describes love that transcends the fairytale love and sexual love of today's society. It describes a love that is consistent and constant through all the trials of life. It describes the love of a parent for their children. Choosing to love through life's ups and downs is often hard but so rewarding. Love is described as trusting God always even to the end and never giving up no matter what. Love is a steady presence in your life. It is the investment that keeps on paying and growing. The more you invest in God, the better your dividends in love. A mother's love keeps on and this description is exactly what a mother's love is.

Mother's Day Legacy
by Donesa Walker
In Honor of My Mother, Teresa White
At the time I knew the mystery of conception was mine, I felt the pennies of love rain down.
In the moment I heard a heartbeat, the love increased my heart's dividend by a pound.
The movement of that tiny body within mine expounded the investment more.
The pains of birth pulled on those strings and boy, was it a chore.
Although the dollars teetered in time, the minutes made more than cents of rhyme.
From the moment those sweet eyes met mine, my heart turned on a dime.
When those sweet hands reached up to my heart requesting my arms to gather them close, I felt my value rise.
When the child came running to me in hurt awaiting my embrace, I cared not one nickel about any other prize.
Though some days, I felt nickeled and dimed, the love still poured forth from me into my growing teens through time.
The years went by and my investment grew uninterrupted by my attention and the days were sublime.
Unawares was I that my harried days and long nights were growing dividends reinvested.
The children grew and drew on me from my monetary wealth...
a constant cost that I should spend unaware of its dividend arrested.
A year went by and then a few, a dollar spent that was not earned. A college degree, then two then three.
Off on their own…until a mate yearned.
A spouse was added then it was two...until the day I got that infamous call...
My grandchild would soon be born...my wealth had grown as I had aged not in the way I thought at all.
My child had another, my heart paid dues...the time/money through the roof shot loose.
My children have doubled my dividend of four, to eight now nine...
for this love that keeps on growing from mine to mine to mine...
My wealth has grown through the years invested while I was poor
into the Hand of God who knew how love paid more than golden ore.
My Children's children are now my investment, a legacy of unbridled wealth.
You see I invested not only in mine but those around me as well.
The pouring of myself into those little children brought dividends of love year after year
though some days the challenges were given,
I walked on in no fear.
As I look back from my aged years and gaze upon my life, I see the investment I made into the future lives.
As markets go up and down, my investment has its moments
but never a day have I had a loss though death has taken its toll,
My investment is laid up in Heaven awaiting my final call.
Wealth shouldn't be measured in monetary means but rather the depths of love .
for in this moment I know I am the wealthiest woman in the world.
You see I know the truth by now, I have a wealth of love.

And that about wraps it up. God is strong, and he wants you strong. So take everything the Master has set out for you, well-made weapons of the best materials. And put them to use so you will be able to stand up to everything the Devil throws your way. This is no afternoon athletic contest that we'll walk away from and forget about in a couple of hours. This is for keeps, a life-or-death fight to the finish against the Devil and all his angels. Be prepared. You're up against far more than you can handle on your own. Take all the help you can get, every weapon God has issued, so that when it's all over but the shouting you'll still be on your feet. Truth, righteousness, peace, faith, and salvation are more than words. Learn how to apply them. You'll need them throughout your life. God's Word is an indispensable weapon. In the same way, prayer is essential in this ongoing warfare. Pray hard and long. Pray for your brothers and sisters. Keep your eyes open. Keep each other's spirits up so that no one falls behind or drops out.
Ephesians 6:10-18

In His Presence... Filled with His Purpose!

In His Presence...Filled with His purpose.
James 4:2 You do not have because you do not ask God.
You ask and do not receive when you ask amiss to spend it on your own pleasure.
Truth, righteousness, peace, faith and salvation: these are the weapons in this warfare. God's word gives us all the tools we will need. Not too long ago I bought my boys a Swiss Army Knife. Boy! were they fascinated with all the different tools & uses but before long, I found it sitting around not being used and then they swapped for a regular pocket knife because they never learned the value in the other tools. As Christians, we often are the same as these little boys. We have tools we do not use because we haven't pulled them out, tried them out and understand their uses. We've discarded them in favor of only a simple tool because we didn't value the fullness of God. We get caught up in the prayer of I need instead of the power of the intercession. We exercise salvation as it is a powerful weapon that keeps the enemy at bay but we never conquer him because we do not employ the full arsenal. Our backs are constantly against the wall fighting against sin/self because we never step into that blessed assurance...of knowing our Savior more....

Paul is writing to the church at Ephesus that using all the weapons from the instruction manual of the Word Of God and consistent prayer, which leads to the practical use of the powerful weapon of righteousness against which there is no law, can conquer the enemy rather than the constant battling on the frontlines. This picture is a picture of tulips growing amongst the bombed out buildings in Ukraine. The flowers that grow in the midst of the war are there because their roots are strong. They do what they are rooted to do no matter the circumstances around them because they are rooted. If we are rooted in the presence of the Lord, knowing the uses of the tools around us, we can produce in the direst of circumstances. We can bloom in beauty in the midst of the greatest wars in our lives because we aren't affected by the bombs but rather rooted in Truth, employed by righteousness and anchored in peace through our faith in Christ Jesus. Our salvation comes through the shedding of His blood on Calvary. That battle has already been won. Center your life on Him. Root, grow deep by using all the tools of this warfare knowing that no matter what the Devil throws at you, God is greater. "In His presence, there's fullness of joy. When we seek to know His heart, we will find such blessed assurance. The ever open door to know our Savior more is in the Presence of the Lord."

45

The first thing I want you to do is pray. Pray every way you know how, for everyone you know. Pray especially for rulers and their governments to rule well so we can be quietly about our business of living simply, in humble contemplation. This is the way our Savior God wants us to live.

Since prayer is at the bottom of all this, what I want mostly is for men to pray—not shaking angry fists at enemies but raising holy hands to God. And I want women to get in there with the men in humility before God, not primping before a mirror or chasing the latest fashions but doing something beautiful for God and becoming beautiful doing it.

1 Timothy 2: 1-3, 8-10

Something Beautiful!

The beauty industry is a multibillion dollar industry because let's face it, we are consumed with our impressions on others. As we approach Mother's Day, we begin to think of all the beauty that there is in a mother and the sacrifices she has made. We honor these precious women on this day as we should, but I want to examine their beauty in the eye of our Creator. So here's my poem based on Timothy's words...the key of beauty to celebrate:

While one may want to think that beauty comes from flawless skin or the perfect figure that one cuts.
The truth is that this beauty is only skin deep and makeup just hides these deep ruts.
The perfect figure is sacrificed in pregnancy and birth,
but the children that stand before us now are way more in worth.
Timothy said it best when he told us the way
It is as simple as taking a moment to simply pray.
Governments, businesses, people and flaws,
God sees our beauty as we pray for all.
Something ugly can be painted nice
If we but take time to pray twice or thrice.
Beauty is said to be in the eye of the beholder.
Isn't it great that God sees me more beautiful when I am older?
You see, my beauty doesn't come from creams nor makeup or even fancy dress.
Beauty comes in the faith in God when I am put through every test.
The trials of motherhood may weigh on this body, making it less in earthly worth,
But the time on my knees spent in prayer makes for beauty that transcends Earth.
So next time you're stressed that you don't look just right, take a moment to spend in prayer,
For the Father whose opinion you really covet will surely meet you there.
He'll wrap you in the finest garment, the one that never fades.
He'll cover your face in His overpowering love and then it will be as he made.
The Master Creator of all of mankind has chosen you for himself,
You are his masterpiece, a thing of rare beauty not to be put on a shelf.
He loves you unconditionally through all of your years, wrinkles and woes.
The purpose he created you for has a heart full of love and ten fingers and toes.
The lemonade you make from each precious lemon is sweetened with sincere prayer.
The Father who loves you more than another sees you as more than fair.
When life gives you lemons and you feel quite bereft, remember His word is true.
The beauty He sees is that of a mom who stays on her knees praying her children through!

Those who think they can do it on their own end up obsessed with measuring their own moral muscle but never get around to exercising it in real life. Those who trust God's action in them find that God's Spirit is in them—living and breathing God! Obsession with self in these matters is a dead end; attention to God leads us out into the open, into a spacious, free life. Focusing on the self is the opposite of focusing on God. Anyone completely absorbed in self ignores God, ends up thinking more about self than God. That person ignores who God is and what he is doing. And God isn't pleased at being ignored.
Romans 8:5-8

God knew what he was doing from the very beginning. He decided from the outset to shape the lives of those who love him along the same lines as the life of his Son. The Son stands first in the line of humanity he restored. We see the original and intended shape of our lives there in him. After God made that decision of what his children should be like, he followed it up by calling people by name. After he called them by name, he set them on a solid basis with himself. And then, after getting them established, he stayed with them to the end, gloriously completing what he had begun.
Romans 8:29-30

That's why I don't think there's any comparison between the present hard times and the coming good times. The created world itself can hardly wait for what's coming next. Everything in creation is being more or less held back. God reins it in until both creation and all the creatures are ready and can be released at the same moment into the glorious times ahead. Meanwhile, the joyful anticipation deepens.
Romans 8:18-21

Resilience or Reliance!

There's a beautiful flower in these pictures. It's called the skeleton flower and it blooms prior to the mayapple in some countries. What makes this simple white flower unique is that in the rain the white color fades clear leaving the framework or "skeleton" of the flower visible to the eye which is usually hidden by the white color. It struck me when I saw its beauty that it is in the watering time that the flower changes colors not in heat or hard conditions but the "self" of the flower is revealed under the flowing of rain water.

We are told that resilience is a necessary skill for survival and one of the most important in success but I have found that the key to resilience is reliance. Most people think resilience is reliance on self and adapting to new situations but I have found that the skeleton of the situation matters.

In Romans 8...such a rich chapter that you could teach on it for a long time...Paul is telling the church in Rome, that has gotten fat in self reliance, that if you become self absorbed then you cannot hear God. You cannot function in the realm of faith because you get so used to self reliance that you have never exercised the resiliency of faith that can move mountains. You become so obsessed with your own moral muscle that you fail to understand that true resilience is God reliance not self reliance. God knew from the beginning what would happen in each and every moment and yet, He holds back all of nature to His timetable. He designed a world intricately balanced and so sensitive to Him that everything in nature hears him and responds to him. Looking at the underside of this hydrangea you can see the details just as you can on the skeleton flower and recognize that the framework of this Creator was intentional. He created us from the dust of the Earth; He breathed life into us from His own breath. Every cell in our body just like everything in nature sits in anxious anticipation of His call....this is why our heart yearns within us...and yet..,we become so obsessed with our own selves that we fail to hear Him when He calls. Our morality measures are so caught up in whether one decision or another is made by a court or a person in government that we look to man to make decisions that only God has the right to make. We become so consumed by our own concerns that we fail to recognize the signals of His returning. We walk a moral high ground not acknowledging that He is the creator of all. It is in His presence when the rain of His anointing touches us that we fade and the truth of who we are is revealed. Storms come in our lives not to teach us resiliency or self reliance but rather to reveal our true character in Him...our skeleton, our framework is of His creation and He calls to us to yield and allow the rain, the sweet fragrant water of life to refresh us, to peel back the color and allow His truth to be revealed in our lives. Your situation and circumstances may be a storm in your life of refining character. Press into the wind of His keeping, allow the water of life to rain down deep into your roots so He can soak you in His love and reveal His framework in your life. You are His. Uniquely designed as every cell in your body, to hear His call as He beckons. Every child from conception no matter how that conception occurs is uniquely His...the yearning you have...is for Him. Storms surround you... are you anchored in Him, rooted in Him, ready to allow the resiliency to be Faith in Him rather than self...let go! Lean in. He's there. God, I am so amazed at your completeness in the smallest details of nature. From the tornadoes to the intricacies of a flower, I see your character. Lord I want to be as the skeleton flower yielded to your presence so that as your rain of anointing falls on me, my true character rooted in you is revealed. Let others see Jesus in me when times get hard. Not self reliance but God reliance...the resiliency of faith in your omnipresence and omniscience. God, I trust in you. Help me in my weakness...to fade to your strength.

Open up before God, keep nothing back;
he'll do whatever needs to be done:
He'll validate your life in the clear light of day
and stamp you with approval at high noon.
Quiet down before God,
be prayerful before him.
Don't bother with those who climb the ladder,
who elbow their way to the top.

God keeps track of the decent folk;
what they do won't soon be forgotten.
In hard times, they'll hold their heads high;
when the shelves are bare, they'll be full.

Wait passionately for God,
don't leave the path.
He'll give you your place in the sun
while you watch the wicked lose it.

Psalms 37: 5-7, 18-19, 34

Open Up, Quiet Down and Wait Passionately!

I have often struggled with conflicting directions because it leaves me feeling confused. I've heard many people over the years say that's one thing about God that frustrates them is the conflicting instructions.
The thing about God is His ways are not our ways and confusion isn't from Him so seeing our way clear must be part of His desire for us. In this verse there are three instructions that David penned in his song.
Instructions on getting in on God's ways.

First he tells us to open up before GOD not man. I'm a very open person but my husband is not. I have nothing to hide from anyone and freely admit who I am, where I am in life and even am open about my errors so I got the open up part down pat! I can freely say that He hears me and has kept His promises in validation and affirmation as I have no doubt in Him....but the Quiet down is my hard...I run hot! I run wide open and the quiet part is hard for me. Being quiet before God almost seems a conflict in instructions to Open Up but it's not. The Quiet is the lead into the Waiting...the quiet is the place of listening. For many years I have worked with children and some of them struggle to control themselves. I have discovered that when quiet descends, it often takes them a little longer to find that self control. In fact, quiet often draws attention to their raucous behavior. Quiet is a place of self reflection first then a place of God reflection. First we look around and notice that things aren't going our way and we holler out drawing attention then in the stillness, we come to understand that the quiet is actually speaking to us to Be still and know that He is God. He sees you, He knows you. I've discovered in the quiet, I can hear Him much better. This is why God tells us to take time away and to come apart. We get so caught up in the noise, making our requests known that we forget the quiet. Last evening as dusk descended and the quiet came, I began to hear the frogs grow louder and louder. They were there all that time but their voices were hidden in the clutter of all the other noise...when the quiet began to descend in the dusk, their calls were overwhelming. I see God trying to talk to us but we cannot hear Him among the clashing sounds around us. In the quiet and the stillness, I can hear Him calling. He is saying to Wait Passionately. Wow! How do those two words go together? I mean I can do a lot of things passionately because I am a person with loud feelings but waiting passionately...how does that work? Passionate waiting requires the training of the stillness, for passionate waiting is a place of strong faith. Abram and Sarah did not wait passionately, they tried to do it their own way and we are still dealing with that mess. In fact, it is hard to find those that did wait passionately in scripture because it is hard to do. Samson learned the hard way to wait passionately because his impulsiveness led to his downfall but in the quiet, he learned to wait passionately and God redeemed him. David was a man of many passions so he is writing this with full knowledge that passionate waiting is tough. He had to learn it. He had many struggles before he learned the lessons of the quiet. This is actually one of my very favorite verses. It has a promise in it that is powerful! "Wait on the Lord, And keep His way, And He shall exalt you to inherit the land; When the wicked are cut off, you shall see it."
Psalms 37:34 NKJV

Passionately waiting requires staying on the path God put before you even when it is rocky and hard. Keep holding on because His promise is that He will exalt you to inherit the land and when others cannot see it, you will see His promises come to fruition. They that wait on The Lord shall renew their strength...in the quiet...they shall mount up with wings as eagles..they shall run and not be weary, they shall walk and not faint. Teach me Lord, train me Lord, to wait.

"Sing, barren woman, who has never had a baby.
Fill the air with song, you who've never experienced childbirth! You're ending
up with far more children than all those childbearing women." God says so!
"Clear lots of ground for your tents! Make your tents large. Spread out! Think
big! Use plenty of rope, drive the tent pegs deep.
You're going to need lots of elbow room
for your growing family. You're going to take over whole nations;
you're going to resettle abandoned cities. Don't be afraid—you're not going to
be embarrassed. Don't hold back—you're not going to come up short.
You'll forget all about the humiliations of your youth,
and the indignities of being a widow will fade from memory.
For your Maker is your bridegroom, his name, God-of-the-Angel-Armies!
Your Redeemer is The Holy of Israel, known as God of the whole earth.
You were like an abandoned wife, devastated with grief,
and God welcomed you back, Like a woman married young
and then left," says your God.

"Afflicted city, storm-battered, unpitied:
I'm about to rebuild you with stones of turquoise,
Lay your foundations with sapphires,
construct your towers with rubies, Your gates with jewels,
and all your walls with precious stones. All your children will have God for their
teacher— what a mentor for your children!
You'll be built solid, grounded in righteousness,
far from any trouble—nothing to fear! far from terror—it won't even come close!
If anyone attacks you, don't for a moment suppose that I sent them,
And if any should attack, nothing will come of it.
I create the blacksmith who fires up his forge and makes a weapon designed to
kill. I also create the destroyer— but no weapon that can hurt you has ever been
forged. Any accuser who takes you to court
will be dismissed as a liar. This is what God's servants can expect.
I'll see to it that everything works out for the best."
God's Decree.

Isaiah 54: 1-6, 11-17

Infertility!

In Biblical times, the value of a woman was in her ability to marry well and have children. Without children, this woman had to do all her tasks herself and she had a small place on the map of her family. She was often pushed aside and another wife taken if she didn't have children quickly. You can only imagine the grief of a barren woman in that culture. Today, we have science and procreative measures which have allowed many who were infertile to have children. We have adoption for those who desire children but cannot conceive but these still do not take away the pain and desire naturally placed within to have children.

The death of a child through miscarriage or pregnancy loss, stillbirth or a child lost early in their life is so heart-rending. The hardest part is often the lack of time in true grieving as everyone expects you to just have another or try again. The loss of a child in our city by a stray bullet into her grandparents' home over this past weekend has awakened many to the issue of violence and yet...that grief, no matter what laws, punishments or other is done, will not be assuaged. Grief for what could've been...grief for the loss...grief for the future which will never be...these are insurmountable many days...and then the nights. Loss is horrendous and there is no way to repay or undo that loss. That grief will always live in the hearts and minds of all of us who have suffered this separation here on earth especially in the shortening of a life in a violent taking. That's where His promise comes in. You see, there is special significance this year and this time as Israel celebrates 74 years as a nation on May 14th. This word from Isaiah is a promise of restoration to the barren woman and a promise of the future for that which was lost. It is a promise from our God to be the husband to the widow, to protect His people and a foreshadowing of His revelation in the church.

It is a call to action to set aside our grief of the future we lost and embrace the preparation of our future in Him. He says to begin to prepare for an abundance. His restoration process is like that of no other.
When the spring rains come to the ground, the abundance of harvest will be profound. When the church waters the ground with her tears of repentance then the harvest will flourish. When we who have grieved so long awaken to the veil being rent and see the reality rather than the illusion, our grief will turn to joy.

God who wipes away every tear is giving a promise that we will bear much fruit and the churches that are the true bride will begin to see His outpouring upon them in the coming days. Church, it is time to arise. Prepare your tents, add the necessary things to prepare for His outpouring. Many lives/souls previously lost will now be awakened and will come hungering for truth and repentance. His time of harvest is nearing. The signs of the times are here.

Lean in as things get rocky. Prepare your hearts to embrace the hurting. Open your arms to the children of God's making. He has gone to prepare a place for you and He is coming soon. To the barren, Prepare your home for children as His blessings will far surpass your expectations. To the hurting, He will bring you peace and will use you through your grief to become a beacon of safety for other children. To the widow, He is calling you to step out into something new with Him as your love, your bridegroom. Greater things He has done. Intercede for our city and our country, repent of your ways that haven't honored Him for today He has an amazing plan beginning for you!

Don't run up debts, except for the huge debt of love you owe each other. When you love others, you complete what the law has been after all along. The law code—don't sleep with another person's spouse, don't take someone's life, don't take what isn't yours, don't always be wanting what you don't have, and any other "don't" you can think of—finally adds up to this: Love other people as well as you do yourself. You can't go wrong when you love others. When you add up everything in the law code, the sum total is love.

Romans 13: 8-10

The Don'ts That Equal The DO!

Math has never been my strong suit but this math is pretty clearly put!
Don't run up debts +
Don't sleep with another's spouse +
Don't take someone's life +
Don't take what isn't yours +
Don't always be wanting what you don't have +
Equals=**Loving other people as well as you love yourself!**
When you add up all the things of God's law it=LOVE!
This is the only place you cannot go wrong! If what you do is done in God's love...
not the twisted sense of "love" that society has imposed.

Happiness defined by God equals Joy which is Jesus, then Others, then You, but happiness defined by society is "have it my way"! You cannot both loan a dollar and borrow a dollar from the same source to get positive. $1-1=0$
Fear plus God's Love equals oneness with God because perfect love casts out fear. Fear of God (known as respect) plus love of God equals LOVE because when you multiply one times one it equals one which is completely aligning in God. But when you fear God, love God, love others and follow God's law then you get Fruitful Love...love that has the ability to feed you and still has seeds to plant and harvest in the lives of yourself and others leading to a crop of continuous growth of Love. You've heard that love conquers all but only God's love truly has that ability because it is the fruitful kind that pays out. Worrying about the things society or men have planned or are doing is not part of that sum. The sum total of love comes from working and thriving within His design. You are His. The fruit of Him. Walk in His love and you will thrive! When you feel your world is caving in, activate His love towards another and watch it begin to multiply in your life. It's the magic multiple. The secret sauce. The fruitful life. It's the DO!

Don't overlook the obvious here, friends. With God, one day is as good as a thousand years, a thousand years as a day. God isn't late with his promise as some measure lateness. He is restraining himself on account of you, holding back the End because he doesn't want anyone lost. He's giving everyone space and time to change.

2 Peter 3: 8-9

Time Is Not On My Side!

The year is 2022. 0-1000 Day 1, 1001-2000 Day 2? So I have 78 years to live like I want, right?
Nope. Let's read it again.
This is Day 3....He rose on the 3rd day at Dawn! That means any day He can come.
Grammar is important. It says WITH God, a day is as good as a thousand years. Not God's day is 1000 man years. So many folks have misconstrued the meaning. The promises of God are true and He isn't late with His promise as we measure lateness...He's holding back and restraining because of you...
He desires to give you one more chance...He wants no one to perish...
This morning I got up at 3 mst and arrived home at noon cst. But I lost time traveling in the air as I crossed time zones. Did I lose the time for real? No. It's a measurement of time in one area that is different than in another and this is the concept being explained here.

God's timing isn't ours. I have friends anxiously awaiting the right spouse, home, job, child, etc. We pray expecting as God instructed us to but the timing is just out of our control and this causes us to make impulsive decisions rather than waiting on God. We get so anxious to make His promise happen that we create future problems for ourselves. I am the first to admit that controlling time needs to be in my wheelhouse because I can get some stuff done when I have the time in my control but God's timing is a "different" time zone! He doesn't observe man's calendar and clock as His but He hears you. He knows your needs and believe it or not, He knows the perfect timing.
I've watched time and again as He has worked and it is amazing.

This past Sunday, I drove to church by myself for the first time since surgery. As I was leaving church a little later than usual due to a wedding celebration, I kept thinking I needed to stop to get Taco Bell. I'm not a big fan so that was a weird thought. I called Wes and he said nay.., but As I was on my way home, I mean the craving for Taco Bell was unbelievable. So I thought I'll just swing by. When I pulled up, there were several cars in front moving slowly and I thought, forget it...but I just couldn't escape this feeling. So I waited, ordered a few tacos then when I got to the window, God told me to pay for the order behind me and tell the cashier God really loved her and He "hears her". Y'all! She burst into tears! What a holy moment I almost missed! She said, about 90 minutes ago, I was just so frustrated that I said God if you really love me and care for me, have a car drive-thru, pay for the meal of the one behind them and tell me that you love ME! Did you catch that? A holy moment. God's timing. I was the tool. If I had dismissed that moment, He would've used someone else but I caught that Holy moment because I listened.

I'm sharing this not to embarrass or for any acclaim. I am sharing because we are surrounded by Holy Moments. We just have to catch them. They are not what we think. We are in His timing...His messengers...His hands extended. He's giving everyone space and time to change...to hear...to be His hands/feet.

Holy moments. That impulse you feel but are just not sure...don't ignore it. Leave space and time for God.

We're here! We've come back to you. You're our own true God! All that popular religion was a cheap lie, duped crowds buying up the latest in gods. We're back! Back to our true God, the salvation of Israel. The Fraud picked us clean, swindled us of what our ancestors bequeathed us, Gypped us out of our inheritance— God-blessed flocks and God-given children. We made our bed and now lie in it, all tangled up in the dirty sheets of dishonor. All because we sinned against our God, we and our fathers and mothers. From the time we took our first steps, said our first words, we've been rebels, disobeying the voice of our God." * * *

Jeremiah 3:22-25

The Fraud!

The hunter watches with delight when the phone pings telling him a deer is in the corn. He clicks on the picture and sees a beautiful large buck has wandered into the feed. Cautiously the deer feeds on that which is not naturally occurring but has called to him through scent and message via the forest. This deer knows that there is danger this time of year but he is lured into a falseness by the enticing scents of other deer and of this wonderful corn. The bait is set, the temptation is there, now all that remains is the hunter being physically present when the deer decides to indulge. The fraud gradually creeps in making a habit lulling the deer into a false sense of security until one day....suddenly he is running for his life, injured and broken towards the water, a place of safety where his scent will be washed away, lost among the forest where he can heal from his brokenness and hurt. He has learned a lesson in life that the water is a place of refreshing and safety, providing solace and refuge.

When we like the deer come to realize that God alone is our heart's desire, our source and our shield then we too come back to the heart of worship in Him. The imposter is all about catching us off guard, luring us into the falseness of politics and policies, passionate debate and coffee shops instead of true worship. We so easily set aside these false convictions at the first scent of something that benefits our flesh instead of clinging to the cross because the path of the cross seems to be dark and lonely, fraught with undesirable traps and seems to be a harder place when the open field of offerings filled with lights, music and crowds beckons us...sure we are stepping out into an open field of target but the social aspect beckons. Yes, we have to give up some things we were raised to believe like the safe parameter of God's laws but this is all about love and friendship and connection. The false doctrine of all roads lead to God, and there are many gods, feels wrong, as well as the other lessons but yet we are ok because we know the truth...we will just tolerate this misstep from this person leading because he's new...soon to realize, as we are running for cover, that the falseness has stolen our inheritance because the lies have infiltrated our children as we fed on the popular religion in the bed of lies while our truth was destroyed and the trap was sprung. We sinned against God in accepting the worship of ourselves instead of Him with every song sung in supposed worship filled with I, me, my instead of Him.

We must get back to the heart of worship where it is truly all about Him! We must run for dear life to The Living Water to repentance and refuge. We must once again reevaluate and reestablish our relationship with The One True God and lay aside our falseness. We must find our place in Him and follow Him as He leads. You see, the forest trail that looked not as good as the open pasture provides a place of green grass to rest beside still waters and The Good Shepherd is there watching over us, providing us with the fruitful acorns and feed that He grows and nourishes because He knows just what we need and when we need it. It is time to listen to the inner voice, turn and run from that which has falsely lured us into the enemy's camp. Get your things, your family and yourself on the road back to God. Rise up, get dressed and find a house of true worship today where He dwells. Go into the Holy of Holies and there repent and be made new again.

God has set his throne in heaven;
he rules over us all. He's the King!
So bless God, you angels,
ready and able to fly at his bidding,
quick to hear and do what he says.
Bless God, all you armies of angels,
alert to respond to whatever he wills.
Bless God, all creatures,
wherever you are—
everything and everyone made by God.
And you, O my soul, bless God!

Psalms 103: 19-22

Bless God!

Bless is an action of endowment of something cherished or favored. Endow is to provide with an ability or asset. God set His throne in Heaven and rules over all of us and yet He gave us Choice. He endowed us with the ability to choose Him! He's the King! In all of history, the King's will surpassed that of the common man. If the King ordered something, the person so ordered must obey. David is King in Israel and He understands this. He understands the order of the universe and who the King of all Kings is as he writes this song. This king on Earth is ordering all of creation not to just worship but to bless the King of glory because He knows that blessing is more than just passive bowing down. Blessing is a choice of giving up that which is most honored and cherished. Blessing is the best of the best. The blessing of God's favor was given in the form of His son's sacrifice of His life. Jesus chose to give His life but God, the King of all Kings had to choose to allow this as He looked down on the pain of His son and heard Him cry out on the cross. The sin that Jesus took disfigured Him but it was that moment of separation that broke Him. He cries out as the sun goes dark and the veil in the Holy of Holies is rent in two...He cries out "My God, My God, why hast thou forsaken me? " because Jesus was completely God and completely man but at that moment the two had to be torn apart. God gave His greatest blessing in the agony of pain as He turned His back on His only son on the cross because Jesus chose to die for our sins. "It is finished" wasn't a declaration of death. It was a declaration of completed blessing. He chose to give His life, His most cherished thing-Himself. God chose to allow it by turning away. There is no greater blessing in the world than a person laying down their life for another in sacrifice except when the King of all Kings chose to allow His Son to give His life freely. It was the one thing He could not bear as He saw the choices into the future. He sees and knows and yet He still blessed us with the ability to bless. What is a blessing?

Choosing to favor someone or something with the best of us, the worst of us, the all of us. A blessing is a choosing to worship, praise, adore and an act of giving ourselves into the keeping of another. Jesus said from the cross, "Father, into your hands I commit my Spirit." This is the moment of His supreme blessing of all mankind because in that moment He gave His greatest blessing into the hands of the Father to be held for us. When the Spirit indwells us, it is the Spirit of God Himself. It is the Spirit which Jesus Himself gave unto the Father for safekeeping. He gave Himself completely in His blessing to us because He was separated completely from God at that moment with the weight of all the sins in the world. And yet, He chose to give you a choice of free will and the ability to bless or curse. What will you do with this supreme gift of Blessing? Will you command your own soul to Bless God as David commanded his soul? You can choose to walk in a life of blessing or a life of cursing. It is your choice. Jesus already made His sacrifice that gave you the ultimate choice. No longer do you have to be bound by the curse of sin that was set in the Garden of Eden as Jesus broke that curse with His sacrifice. I choose this day to Bless God. I choose this minute and every minute of every day to Bless God with all that I am. I choose through the hard times and the good times to Bless God. Blessings from above are gifts from His storehouse and He is gracious and merciful to us in His blessings when we choose to live and walk the Blessed Life.

"Come. Sit down. Let's argue this out."
This is God's Message:
"If your sins are blood-red,
they'll be snow-white.
If they're red like crimson,
they'll be like wool.
If you'll willingly obey,
you'll feast like kings.
But if you're willful and stubborn,
you'll die like dogs."
That's right. God says so.

Isaiah 1: 18-20

Written in Red!

Red-Crimson Tide-Blood
Red symbolizes LOVE, we use it on Valentine's, we send red roses that signify passion...
Scarlet is a color of red that represents sin, especially sexual sin..as in The Scarlet Letter, the red light districts,
Harlots in the Bible wore Scarlet and in the early 1900s wearing red lipstick or clothing meant you had loose
morals....Now wearing red at times means the heart...as in supporting Heart Health.

The point is that Red represents different things in different times to different people.
In China red is happiness, in Russia it's the color of Communism...For hundreds of years, red and green have
been the traditional colors of Christmas...Green, for example, represents the eternal life of Jesus Christ, just as
evergreen trees remain green the whole winter long. Likewise, red represents the blood shed by Jesus Christ
during his crucifixion. Crimson is a color of red that is close to purple and it denotes victory & praise. In letters
of Crimson God wrote His love on a hillside so long, long ago...for you and for me Jesus died and Love's greatest story was told. I love you. I love you that's what Calvary said...I love you, I love you...I love you written in red.

Who is this that cometh from Edom, with dyed garments from Bozrah? this that is glorious in his apparel, traveling in the greatness of his strength? I who speak in righteousness, mighty to save. Isaiah 63:1

Crimson-Written in Red
Red symbolizes power in both politics and wealth.
Nahum 2:3 The shield of his mighty men is red; his soldiers are clothed in scarlet. The chariots come with flash-
ing metal on the day he musters them; the cypress spears are brandished.
"And they stripped Him and put a scarlet robe on Him. When they had twisted a crown of thorns, they put it on
His head, and a reed in His right hand. And they bowed the knee before Him and mocked Him, saying,
"Hail, King of the Jews!""
Matthew 27:28-29 NKJV

Future-false flag

Rev 12:3 And another sign appeared in heaven: behold, a great red dragon, with seven heads and ten horns,
and on his heads seven diadems.

"Get out of bed, Jerusalem!
Wake up. Put your face in the sunlight.
God's bright glory has risen for you.
The whole earth is wrapped in darkness,
all people sunk in deep darkness,
But God rises on you,
his sunrise glory breaks over you.
Nations will come to your light,
kings to your sunburst brightness.
Look up! Look around!
Watch as they gather, watch as they approach you:
Your sons coming from great distances,
your daughters carried by their nannies.
When you see them coming you'll smile—big smiles!
Your heart will swell and, yes, burst!
All those people returning by sea for the reunion,
a rich harvest of exiles gathered in from the nations!
And then streams of camel caravans as far as the eye can see,
young camels of nomads in Midian and Ephah,
Pouring in from the south from Sheba,
loaded with gold and frankincense,
preaching the praises of God.
And yes, a great roundup
of flocks from the nomads in Kedar and Nebaioth,
Welcome gifts for worship at my altar
as I bathe my glorious Temple in splendor.

Isaiah 60: 1-7

Heart Swell!

When someone says, my heart swells, they are proud, happy and overjoyed! In these scriptures, Isaiah is speaking of a future time for Israel when all the Earth is struggling but God brings favor upon Israel such that all of the ancestral draw brings the descendants back home to her shores. It is a time when Israel, especially the city of Jerusalem, reigns in splendor and oozes success. It is a time of rejoicing and preparation also. Notice that Isaiah instructs them to get out of bed and face the sunlight. He compares this time of rejoicing to the coming of a day-a very special day-but using this as an illustration of how one must be prepared to see the coming of the day. Watching the day rise at dawn is especially beautiful because as the first streams of light break, you can visualize the beauty. God wants us to wake up and begin to see the rays of Sonshine in our world. He wants us to see the breaking dawn in our situations and not be focused on the night. On winter days, especially rainy ones where the sun rarely breaks through the clouds, it is hard to get up and get going unless you are disciplined and purposeful.

The night, the cold, the rain calls you to snuggle in and stay where you feel warm and rested but it is time that we break out of our cocoons of contentment and begin to stretch towards His coming. We must wake up to see the rising Son! We must begin to embrace the coming of Jesus with our eyes wide open to what is happening in the world and the signs of His return. Did you know that the temple is beginning to be rebuilt and that the priests are gathering in Jerusalem and have already bought red heifers for sacrifice? These are details given to us as signs of Christ's return. Time to rub the sleep from your eyes, prepare your heart and share His glory. Get out into the dawn of His glory. People across the earth are wrapped in darkness but you can see the streaks of His dawn and you have the opportunity to shake them awake to His presence.
Jesus is coming soon!

"Don't let this rattle you. You trust God, don't you? Trust me. There is plenty of room for you in my Father's home. If that weren't so, would I have told you that I'm on my way to get a room ready for you? And if I'm on my way to get your room ready, I'll come back and get you so you can live where I live. And you already know the road I'm taking."

"If you love me, show it by doing what I've told you. I will talk to the Father, and he'll provide you another Friend so that you will always have someone with you. This Friend is the Spirit of Truth. The godless world can't take him in because it doesn't have eyes to see him, doesn't know what to look for. But you know him already because he has been staying with you, and will even be in you!

"The person who knows my commandments and keeps them, that's who loves me. And the person who loves me will be loved by my Father, and I will love him and make myself plain to him."

John 14: 1-4, 15-17, 21

The Naked Truth!

I love the beauty of the first snow! The gorgeous white blanket that covers everything changing its look to one of continuity and undefined boundaries. It hides the beauty and the ugly under the same covering making it all seem beautiful and new. This is how Christ Jesus describes salvation as being made white as snow...covered by the blanket of His sacrifice, all looks new and beautiful, fresh and unfettered. In this passage, Jesus instructed His disciples to not be rattled or upset by things coming to pass as God intends it but rather to trust Him and reside in/with the Spirit of Truth. I love the kids' book, The Emperor's New Clothes because it is such a statement of today's society. The news media screams their own version of things despite what we see & know much like the "tailors" of the Emperor in the story. They project a version that even the demented emperor begins to believe so much that he strips down naked walking the streets with people bowing and buying into the lie they were told for fear of being judged by others to be less than. That fear made them foolish. Then a child who is full of innocence breaks the silence by declaring the truth and suddenly eyes are opened. The truth was there the whole time abiding right before their eyes but they refused to see it because they let fear make them weak and ineffective. When the snow begins to melt, all of the beauty of that Holy Moment is suddenly revealing of the Truth in our lives. That is when we take a look of Truth and begin to change and clean up the landscape of our existential life so that true beauty can reign. Changes must be made in us as revealed by the Spirit of Truth so that we may continue to walk in the Holy Moments of purity with Him.

Often these are hard truths revealing the lies and deceit of others when we suddenly realize we are naked walking before a crowd who bought into the lies even though they too could see the truth if they had only fully looked. Walking in the Spirit of Truth means exchanging the naked lies of this world for a robe of pure anointing given by the Savior of the world. He came as a child declaring the Truth. He went to the cross declaring the Truth and providing covering for our nakedness. He rose again declaring the Truth of what He had promised and He left us a covering, a robe, a Spirit of Truth to cloak us in His righteousness. He will come again very soon to declare His own-those who walk in the Spirit of Truth. The persons who love Him, love the Father and abide in the Spirit of Truth so they cannot be fooled by the deceit of this godless world. Jesus is preparing a place for us. He is freshening the decor and taking care of the last details for His bride. He's coming back just like He said He would. Take off the blinders that declare this world as your home. See the naked truth that He has covered you with His own sacrifice in His peace. Don't be rattled by the world and the circumstances. You are nothing but a naked person walking around in the lies of the world without His covering, but with His Spirit of Truth comes a covering of peace!

"There's trouble ahead when you live only for the approval of others, saying what flatters them, doing what indulges them. Popularity contests are not truth contests—look how many scoundrel preachers were approved by your ancestors! our task is to be true, not popular.
"To you who are ready for the truth, I say this: Love your enemies. Let them bring out the best in you, not the worst. When someone gives you a hard time, respond with the supple moves of prayer for that person. If someone slaps you in the face, stand there and take it. If someone grabs your shirt, giftwrap your best coat and make a present of it. If someone takes unfair advantage of you, use the occasion to practice the servant life. No more payback. Live generously.

Luke 6: 26-30

Supple Prayer!

After multiple back surgeries, I can say without a doubt that my movement has been less than supple. Supple movement is flexible movement with ease from practice and automatic movement. As I recently started back exercising, every muscle in my body has screamed in frustration and disuse letting me know of the objection but with consistency, I am seeing better movement in my back and body. It's easy to stay in the place where you are and grow stagnant in Him. It is much easier to sit quietly or trust than to exercise Faith which sometimes doesn't perform as imminently as you desire. Sitting in my recliner relaxed is much easier on my back than exercise but by doing so I limit my future potential. When we train and exercise our bodies, it results in automatic supple movements of flexible ease because our bodies are used to that and it doesn't startle them or overuse them past the point of comfort. When we train and exercise our prayer life, it results in supple and confident prayer that exercises our Faith automatically causing change because we are expecting it. When you exercise truth, you move in truth. When you exercise love, you move in love. When you are fully exercised in these things, hard times don't cause the breakdown, instead you respond with supple prayer of faith and walk it out in love. Popularity isn't Truth. Hard times bring out the truth just like hard exercise makes you more supple. Why? Because when you go through tough times, you are much more likely to exercise your prayer life until it is a supple or automatic movement for your response. In schools, we train kids on fire drills because we want their response to be an automatic response not a fear response should the occasion truly occur. We prepare for the worst by exercising the response in a non threatening training. Our prayer life should be constant as scripture tells us that effective and fervent prayer gains much in the eyes of God because we pray as He would desire when we are in joint movement with Him. Supple prayer leads to living generously in love. It is a move of practice and automaticity. When you do something often, such as brushing your teeth when you first wake up...you don't think about it...you just do it. It is an automated process to your body because you trained yourself. It still must be done consciously and consistently to have effect but the purpose is preventing a future issue of cavities while also resulting in nice breath and a clean mouth. But if you brush only once per day, quickly the bacteria from food and life end up back on your teeth's surface and in your body. Brushing after every meal and morning and night is important to true dental health. The truth is that very few people I know exercise this principle because it is inconvenient. The same is true with prayer.

Prayer changes things and is so powerful but we must make time for it and or practice it for it to become a supple part of our life. It takes delivery discipline and focused purpose to set time aside to read the word and pray. It takes intention to stop in your daily life and laser focus on prayer, but the rewards are amazing. Just like my body is more supple and graceful with a few weeks of daily exercise and my teeth are strong with fresh breath because I brush them multiple times per day, my prayer is supple because I engage in it constantly as a form of worship. Try it. Practice it. Engage in prayer and worship as a lifestyle habit so that you can respond in supple prayer when someone hurts you rather than in the unkind way they did. Practicing Prayer doesn't mean you won't fall or have problems. It means that when you do, for you surely will, you will roll with it and get up easily dusting yourself off instead of breaking something in you. Supple movement of prayer has double benefits. If you practice on your knees, the up/down movement will be good for your body too!

So, my very dear friends, don't get thrown off course. Every desirable and beneficial gift comes out of heaven. The gifts are rivers of light cascading down from the Father of Light. There is nothing deceitful in God, nothing two-faced, nothing fickle. He brought us to life using the true Word, showing us off as the crown of all his creatures.

James 1: 16-18

Rivers of Light!

I love waterfalls. I think they are one of the most beautiful things in nature. I find peace in just hearing the water ebb/flow at the beach too. God is more pure than water. You see, water is a filter of the best kind. It washes away anything but it also carries things from one place to another. It is a powerful force that is almost beyond our imaginings. We harness its power to make energy. We must have water to survive. Our bodies are aqueous and our brains use 80% of our liquid intake daily. James instructs the church to not be distracted by that which is happening around them. He warns them to stay on course and follow the light because every good and desirable thing comes from The Father out of Heaven. He says the gifts are rivers of light cascading down reminding me of the sparkling diamonds of water I see in a waterfall. Every drop of water is essential but the value of water is higher in the places it is hard to get. River water is free but that same water has a price when pumped into your home and a higher price when it is bottled and higher still when that bottle is in a location where liquids are controlled like an airport. The water is the same but the delivery is not. The Father of Light sends blessings to us as waterfalls of blessings but most are unrecognized and ignored because they are taken for granted until they are limited in scope like the bottled water. Health isn't appreciated as much until it is challenged and wealth isn't looked upon as a gift by the wealthy. Things that do not have a price or are Free are often ignored as not as valuable when in reality they have extreme value. Salvation is free to all who accept it but only because the price has already been paid. The truth is that there is no such thing as freedom except a price is paid to maintain it by those who sacrifice their lives in our military service.

Think back to creation...Scripture based truth. God spoke the word Light and the sun was formed to control or hold the Light just like the stars. These are free gifts from the Father of Light that we see each day/night yet how often do we thank God for the sun, moon, stars, etc? God isn't a fickle God. He created these things to control our world, our temperature and our seasons. The gifts that come down in rays of sunshine we rarely acknowledge as we bemoan the things we do not have. We get so caught up in the ME that we forget the magnificent balance of all creation and our place. He spoke most things into motion but each of us is God breathed into existence. Read that again! He brought us into life through the true Word. He didn't speak us into existence but carefully formed us in our mother's womb fearfully and wonderfully then breathed the breath of life into us. You are the crown of all His creatures and creation. He sets such value on you that He hears you when you call. If you truly grasp the magnificence of the statement, it will leave you breathless. God himself is a river of life cascading down into you and through you when you allow Him access to yourself but He gave you a gift of choice. There is no deceit in Him, nothing less than true face value. He doesn't trick you. He is what He is and has always been and always will be. He is Love! A river of light flowing down through you. Many people bottle it, package it and charge for it but it is free because He already paid the price with His supreme love. Take a minute to begin to appreciate all the goodness God has provided for you. Once you start seeing the water droplets of gifts then you begin to see the waterfall of love and provision. Dive into His light of love cascading down just for you! It will change your life!

As silver in a crucible and gold in a pan,
so our lives are refined by God.

Receiving a gift is like getting a rare gemstone;
any way you look at it, you see beauty refracted.

Friends love through all kinds of weather,
and families stick together in all kinds of trouble.

A cheerful disposition is good for your health;
gloom and doom leave you bone-tired.

The one who knows much says little;
an understanding person remains calm.

Proverbs 17: 3, 8, 17, 22, 27

Beauty Refracted!

A diamond starts out as coal, a golden ring starts out as a rock in the ground, silver starts out as a mineral deposit in the Earth and man started out as dust. Nothing beautiful comes without the work of the creator or maker. Each piece of art, object or person must go through a refining process to become what it is. This photo is a picture of space and the beauty of creation in the making. Our lives are like this. They are beauty in the process but sometimes the process is painful, long and hard. Troubles come, storms rage, and sometimes we get stuck in the muck of life spinning our wheels and getting nowhere! This is all a part of the refining. A piece of coal must go through a lot of darkness (gloom and doom) and incredible pressure to become a diamond and not all coal becomes a diamond. Not all diamonds become works of art or things of beauty either. It is a rare gemstone that becomes a work of art that demonstrates beauty every way you see it. The perfect diamond is beautiful in dark times and is prone to catch the slightest light, but in daylight, the sparkle is irresistible! It refracts the beauty of itself and its creator/designer and setting from every direction. It catches every single piece of light it can, refracting it around to other places and people. This is what we are called to be. God is taking us through a refining process as silver and breaking/sifting us in the pan of life as gold. He is burning away the dross of the ME in the process so that we can be the gift of the rare gemstone/diamond in the setting He has placed us. The key to this is reflection of Him and refraction of His light. Finding beauty in the ashes of life requires a spirit of cheer in hard circumstances. It isn't easy but it is better for your health as being down and out about everything wears a person down and all the people around them too. No circumstances are perfect! There is no one in this world whose life is perfect! Every life has its storms and weather and every life has a refining process because God wants us to achieve pure beauty and devotion to Him the Creator of all things.

One of the rare known facts about diamonds is that they develop in lots of colors ranging from colorless to faintest of pinks to the deepest black. Colored diamonds comprise only 0.01% of the total diamonds mined worldwide. Their rarity makes them immensely valuable. Red diamonds are the rarest and some of the most expensive in the world, then blue like the Hope diamond, then green, then orange, then pink, then yellow to colorless. Each color has a different value based on its abilities such as conducting electricity and its novelty but all diamonds start out as nothing important. A diamond in the rough is valuable because of its form but even after enduring all the storms and pressure and darkness, a diamond doesn't have all the value yet. Next it must go through the cutting and designing which can break and destroy it. Most of the diamonds we see and possess are actually just broken pieces off a truly superior diamond. We are but a piece of a masterpiece and yet we are important. Look at this beauty of space and imagine it as the making. Thousands of years in one glance by a telescope powered by a diamond that was thousands of years in the making. Your purpose is unknown to you but in the hand of The Creator and Designer, you are a masterpiece with great purpose. You are being made, chosen, refined and designed. You are being placed in the perfect setting for you to achieve the purpose He has for you. You may not feel like your purpose is grand or even important but He has great things for you! You may feel like you are nothing more than a piece of rock or an unimportant and overlooked piece of coal but He has grand things for you. Begin to seek His light with every pressure and disappointment. Search and seek Him with all of you! The Hubble telescope doesn't just see the visible spectrum that our eyes can see, it can also see the near-ultraviolet and near-infrared parts of the spectrum. This photo is genuine but it isn't what you would see because your eyes do not have the refraction power of that telescope. It simply has light that you cannot see with your eyes converted to light that you can see with your eyes. The power of the Spirit is that through Him we can see beyond what our eyes can see and He can convert the things we cannot see into images our hearts can see through His word. This is the gift of God like a rare diamond. It has many facets made by the eons of time in the Creator's hand. This gift is yours. This rare, impossible gift is yours. This ability to refract beauty and cheer to all around you is yours simply by seeking His light. The facets or faces of a diamond come because the designer sees the way to cut it to allow the light to refract the deepest, giving it the greatest beauty, but this process is tedious and tiring and extremely stressful to the diamond and the designer, for it is in this moment that the diamond can lose itself in value. You can begin a unique journey to reveal your true beautiful self but you must submit to the designer so that your facets can be revealed. The flawless and perfect red diamond of Jesus' has already made its mark on the world. He submitted His will to that of The Father and became the sacrifice. He now sits on the throne at the right hand of God Himself beckoning us to endure the process so we can become the jewels He desires us to be.

O my soul, bless God.
From head to toe,
I'll bless his holy name!
O my soul, bless God,
don't forget a single blessing!
He forgives your sins–every one.
He heals your diseases–every one.
He redeems you from hell–
saves your life!
He crowns you with love and
mercy–a paradise crown.
He wraps you in goodness–
beauty eternal.
He renews your youth–you're always
young in his presence.

Psalms 103: 1-5

The Paradise Crown!

A crown is set with precious and rare jewels that are meant to adorn a King's head. They are the best of the best because a king is the highest honor in a kingdom. This set of verses keeps coming back to me over and over as if God is stressing this. Each time I read it and meditate on it, I see a different nuance in what He is saying, like a beautiful facet of a diamond being developed and formed by the designer. The crown of life and mercy-Jesus, left His throne in the Heavens to come down to Earth as a mortal man, sacrificing His very life for all mankind-this was the redemption from hell that saved our lives through the forgiveness of our sins. When a king goes to his coronation, he is wrapped in a cloak that signifies his covering and given a crown and scepter to acknowledge his authority. Look at this! This King of Glory came down from above in a baby's form living a life among us, sacrificing Himself for us, but even more, He renews us and restores us into His place of royalty through the placement of the cloak of Beauty eternal and goodness that He wraps us in-as our covering of authority and authenticity. Then He crowns us when we should be crowning Him! He crowns us with a paradise crown of love and mercy!

This is the authority that we walk in daily. We walk in His mercy, goodness and love. I watched a video recently again of the day the announcer made a mistake when crowning Miss Universe and as she was celebrating the win, he spoke up saying wait, I made a mistake, you are the runner up and the other girl is the winner. She is stripped of her crown and roses and cloak-laid bare in embarrassment before an audience and a televised world. I cannot imagine how completely traumatic that must have been. She had worked so hard, believed that she had gained the crown then lost it all because of an error on a piece of paper. It was never hers but had been given to her in error. God doesn't make these mistakes. He chose us for the crown, knowing our flaws and failures. He offers us the Paradise Crown of love and mercy for all of time and with it comes eternal youth in His presence but only in His presence.

You see, some will walk away, taking the crown off because they want the world and what it offers more. Others will keep the crown but leave His presence to have a pity party about their dreams not being granted in their time. Some will sacrifice a jewel from the crown not realizing it's long term value but will sell the love of God or His mercy for fame and fortune on tv. The Paradise Crown is rare. The jewels in it are the finest that the universe has and worth more than anything in this earth-land, money, fame, power and authority. The authority that that crown gives and the covering are offered to each of us for one thing-remaining in His presence. Everyone is looking for the fountain of youth when He has already told us where it is-some just don't like the answer because they want the power/prestige without the sacrifice. Wrapped in Him-cloaked in His goodness and walking always in His light with His Paradise Crown of Love and Mercy upon our brow...this is the Fountain of Youth. For Only In His presence is the fullness of joy.

When God made his promise to Abraham, he backed it all the way, putting his own reputation on the line. He said, "I promise that I'll bless you with everything I have—bless and bless and bless!" Abraham stuck it out and got everything that had been promised to him. When people make promises, they guarantee them by appeal to some authority above them so that if there is any question that they'll make good on the promise, the authority will back them up. When God wanted to guarantee his promises, he gave his word, a rock-solid guarantee—God can't break his word. And because his word cannot change, the promise is likewise unchangeable.

We who have run for our very lives to God have every reason to grab the promised hope with both hands and never let go. It's an unbreakable spiritual lifeline, reaching past all appearances right to the very presence of God where Jesus, running on ahead of us, has taken up his permanent post as high priest for us, in the order of Melchizedek.

Hebrews 6: 13-20

Lifeline of Promise!

When I was a young adult, there was a television game show called "Who wants to be a millionaire?" and during the show the person could call another person as their lifeline if they didn't know the answer to the question. Their life was never in any danger but their game success could depend on whether that person gave good advice or knew the answer. When we get into places of confusion or trouble, we often reach out to the people around us who might assist us such as doctors when we are sick or other mothers for advice, or bankers for financial assistance. When we need a loan, we might require a co-signer, someone to back up our paying ability. I have had many people come to me as a "lifeline" in educational issues for court or school advice as well as some ask me to assist them in spiritual matters or even some in physical advice since I've had some experience there too. The point is that when your back is to a wall, you reach out to people you trust who are there for you or able to help. God's promises are true lifelines. We can trust them as they have been tested and found to be true. When God makes a promise, He fulfills it. When people make a promise, they say "you have my word on it" meaning to trust them and they will honor their promise. But people fail. Their word is only as good as they are and as long as they have the ability to fulfill it..,God's promise isn't dependent on others as He knows our limitations. God's promise is His word that has never failed. If you live, walk, sleep and act in His promises, they are your existence rather than your last resort. In Hebrews, the promised hope is called the unbreakable lifeline. Like the line that holds a mountain climber to the side of the mountain preventing them from falling, it is anchored in a rock, a firm foundation. The anchor of these promises is in The Rock that never moves. God said to Abraham, I promise to bless you with everything I have-through your children and your children's children and as far off as the seas, meaning that His promises don't end. His promises are eternal and true. So since God never breaks His promises and His word is solid lasting infinitely, why do we walk in our own chaos instead of walking in His promise? Why do we let our own situations overwhelm us until we reach out to our earthly lifelines in despair rather than claiming and walking in His promises? I saw a post recently of a woman who brought her husband's shirts to church every service for years and prayed over them for His salvation and Her promise by God her Father was fulfilled: When you seek me with all your heart, you will find me.

Yesterday in our service, I was challenged to begin to walk and claim promise in my life more than I ever have before. Seek the promises God has made in scripture and begin to claim them as yours walking in the truth. I have a promise that God has given me through the many promises in His word and I stand in that promise. Things may look rough sometimes but that's when you anchor in His promise. You may feel like the world has failed and God isn't hearing you. You may feel lost and grieved and totally at loose ends. Reach out for His lifeline of promises, tie a knot and hang on because He hears you, He sees you and He is with you no matter how bad it seems. He will take you through this trial too. He will guide you and direct you. Claim that promise that you are standing on. Say it over and over. Know that He is God and Be still in your Faith in Him. The Rock won't move. His word is strong. He is trustworthy and His lifeline is everything. Grab ahold of God with both hands and never let go. The earthquake may rage around you as it did for all the ancestors in scripture but we can see the end. We get to read the end of the book and know His word is true, everlasting and strong. It will not waver, though the sun turn dark and the moon to blood, His word will not return void. Hold on. His promises are your lifelines and they will stand the test! Search the scripture and pray! Find your promises and hold onto them with all that is in you which is enough because He that is in you is greater than he that is in the world. Create mental scripture pictures. When that adversary comes at you...claim them. How did Jesus fight temptation, by the Word. It is written....God's word created the very world we exist in. He said Let there be...and it is, so you can trust that His word works mighty things. Jesus is at the top of the mountain you are facing and He is holding out the lifeline for you to grab onto in your grief and hurt, pain and confusion. Reach out. Claim His promises--grab the lifeline that is anchored in Him.

Blessed are the undefiled in the way,
Who walk in the law of the Lord!
Blessed are those who keep His
testimonies,
Who seek Him with the whole heart!
They also do no iniquity;
They walk in His ways.
You have commanded us
To keep Your precepts diligently.
Oh, that my ways were directed
To keep Your statutes!
Then I would not be ashamed,
When I look into all Your commandments.
I will praise You with uprightness of heart,
When I learn Your righteous judgments.

Psalms 119: 1-7

Joyful Recharge!

I came home one night a couple of weeks ago and my husband was on a ladder trying to take batteries out of every smoke alarm upstairs and figure out which one was beeping every few seconds. We tried closing the doors and finally pinpointed the sound to my son's room but he was gone. Kept hearing it even with the battery removed so I shut myself in the room and followed the noise to the source which turned out to be a carbon monoxide detector plugged in a low place under a desk area. The battery was low so it was calling out letting us know so we could replace and recharge it. We have been given a task-charged to keep His commandments carefully and for our actions to consistently reflect His decrees so we will not be ashamed by falling short but when we go on and on without recharging fully, we become depleted. The joy is sucked out of us because we begin to perform life and soon we are compromising with evil unintentionally. Joy doesn't come from outside but rather the filling of Him inside. Psalms tells us that being joyful or blessed comes when we seek Him with all our hearts and follow His laws/instructions with integrity. Integrity is doing what you should when no one is watching. To have joy, you seek Him who fills you and you follow His instructions even if no one knows what you are doing or why you do it. The battery in the carbon monoxide detector got low and the detector said, wait I have no more juice so I need to use what power I have left to call out to the people who will replenish my source. This is us! We need a re-charge. We need more joy. We need to seek The Source and cry out that we need replenishment so He will hear us as He promised to do when we seek Him with all our hearts. I honestly haven't even looked at that carbon monoxide detector since I plugged it in who knows how long ago. It was doing its job until it wore out and needed a recharge. God is always ready to fill us and keep us full as He is our source but we must come before Him and let Him know our needs-though He truly knows before we ask-He wants to hear you. He wants you to stay continuously plugged in so that your source is constantly full of joy which allows you to share His light with others. God doesn't ever run out. His joy is complete and full but we must rejoice to stay tapped into Him as our source of power, energy and joy. If you feel life has stolen and used up all your joy, scream out incessantly to The Source and He will hear you and fill you to overflowing once again. God, the circumstances of life keep stealing my joy, please fill me with your overwhelming love so I might float in your joyful waves and rest in your presence. Then I will be recharged, to minister in my workplace of ministry once again.

God claims Earth and everything in it,
God claims World and all who live on it.
He built it on Ocean foundations,
laid it out on River girders.
Who can climb Mount God?
Who can scale the holy north-face?
Only the clean-handed,
only the pure-hearted;
Men who won't cheat,
women who won't seduce.
God is at their side;
with God's help they make it.
This, Jacob, is what happens
to God-seekers, God-questers.

Psalms 24: 1-6

God Quest!

    I have several friends who are mountain climbers and love scaling the mountain and claiming the victory at the summit. I have climbed a few in my younger years and it is a very rewarding feeling to know that you made it. I imagine it is the same feeling for those who finally make their entrance to that city of pearly gates, jasper walls and golden streets. God has claimed this Earth and all that is in it by His creation of it as He claims all the world. Our planet is built by His words alone and yet so infinitely perfect in its land masses surrounded by oceans and girded by rivers. He has set forth a Mountain to climb in our lives that isn't a mountain of physical appearance but of the spiritual realm. David called it Mount God! The north face of a mountain is usually tougher and not for the faint of heart because of the winds that have made it more of a challenge. The north face is the one that has the most difficulty because over thousands of years, steep slopes that receive more sunlight are slowly changed by the freeze/thaw cycle to become less extreme, while northern faces are less likely to experience this so they remain steep and can even be held together by permafrost like glue.

    David calls it the Holy North Face meaning who can climb the challenging mountain of God facing the hardest challenges in life? Only those who are clean of hands, pure of heart, not cheaters and seducers. Only those with God on their side who have God's help to make it. These are the God seekers or God questers. These are those who put God first. I imagine Job is an example of a God quester who climbed the north face of Mount God. He endured unheard of challenges and met them face on, confident in God. And God rewarded him greatly. Most of us are ready to throw in the towel at the first sign of struggle but the north face continues to present challenges all the way to the summit. I have known a few people in my life who are diligently facing and scaling the Holy north face of Mount God. They climb and lean in. They reach out constantly to others below them even when it makes their own climb harder. They are completely pure of heart and clean in their hands doing only what is right. These are those who will arrive at the summit in celebration and glory. I can just imagine the parade in Heaven for them of all who have gone before welcoming them. How do they climb this challenging path? With God. He's always there. He's gone before us. He is our anchor in the rock that holds our climbing ropes and He is there to stabilize us when the winds rail at us. He is there to haul us up when we are weary. He is there when we feel like giving up. He is there calling down words of encouragement and lifting us. He is there cheering us onward and preparing the reward. The quest may be hard but the summit is worth the climb. So hold on and keep climbing!

I'm thanking you, God, from a full heart,
I'm writing the book on your wonders.
I'm whistling, laughing, and jumping for joy;
I'm singing your song, High God.

God holds the high center,
he sees and sets the world's mess right.
He decides what is right for us earthlings,
gives people their just deserts.
God's a safe-house for the battered,
a sanctuary during bad times.
The moment you arrive, you relax;
you're never sorry you knocked.

Psalms 9: 1-2, 7-10

Just Desserts!

Dessert is my favorite part of the meal as it is often a celebration or a reckoning of deliciousness. The meal sustains but the dessert rewards. In Psalms, David says he is writing the book on God's wonders and as he does his heart is full of thankfulness causing him to whistle, laugh and jump for joy as he sings to God. David was taking in his meal by writing God's book but the dessert was just there in the midst of the meal tasting like Heaven. David has just come from battle and has seen God perform. He has seen that the battle belongs to God and all he must do is be there and be willing to take God's instruction. God holds the high center, the place of judgment. He sees all and knows all. He decides what to allow or not allow and He will do all things right, giving dessert of the right portion to all. When someone uses the phrase "just desserts", it means the correct reward or exacting punishment for their choices. When things are tough and you just need a place to rest and relax, God says pull up a seat and let me get you some cake and coffee. He is your sanctuary of safety and your place of comfort. Thanksgiving is a mindset of gratefulness that comes from a place of understanding. It wells up within you when you contemplate the goodness of God and his fruits. In the hardest of times, when you come into the sanctuary of His word and sit down in the chair He has pulled up for you. You can take in a meal of vast wonder in His word and suddenly there's that dessert. That piece of word that is so sweet it sings music to your soul. You just want to dance and sing because it is so yummy! It is a celebration of His goodness and His wonder. He prepares this table for you in the presence of your enemies and your places of darkness/lostness. He knows the path you walk and He is waiting in the sanctuary for you to knock, for He is ready with your meal of goodness and growth along with your just dessert. What portion of God and His word are you seeking?

Are you diving into His word with gladness? The dessert is waiting piled high with the whipped cream of His goodness waiting on you to knock and enter His place of fulfillment.

For my part, I am going to boast about nothing but the Cross of our Master, Jesus Christ. Because of that Cross, I have been crucified in relation to the world, set free from the stifling atmosphere of pleasing others and fitting into the little patterns that they dictate. Can't you see the central issue in all this? It is not what you and I do—submit to circumcision, reject circumcision. It is what God is doing, and he is creating something totally new, a free life! All who walk by this standard are the true Israel of God—his chosen people.
Peace and mercy on them!

Galatians 6: 14-16

Free Life!

When I was growing up there was a movie called Free Willy about a killer whale/orca who was in captivity as a trained orca but he wanted to be truly free. He was trained to perform and he had all his needs met but he wanted the freedom of the ocean rather than the water park he was kept in. Sometimes we get so wrapped up in the performance of the tricks to stay in this game of Life that we forget Jesus came and died so we might have life abundant. We are no longer subject to the laws of Moses with all the strictures but we walk in freedom with our Savior. What is this freedom? It is free from the dictates of man and built on a relationship with the One who did the work on the cross. Freedom is a mindset not a position. You can be free in any situation if your heart is in Christ Jesus and you can be in bondage in any situation if your heart is unanchored. Paul in writing to the Galatians was talking about being bound by the Jewish laws of Moses involving circumcision rather than the freedom in Jesus. It's not about whether you do or you don't do a particular thing but rather how you walk in a relationship. Relationships require commitment and communication to thrive. Freedom in a relationship means that I am willing to give to the other person the whole of me, trusting them to also be as open and free with me as I am with them. It is the anchor of trust/faith that brings freedom. Being anchored in Jesus means I am giving all of me and trusting that all of Him is available to me. When I chose to marry my husband, I didn't say I'll marry you but withhold this part of myself for my own delight. I gave all that I am into his trust as he committed all of himself to me. The freedom of that Lifestyle means there is an intimacy there of completely knowing the other person. If someone tells me he did this or that, I know the truth because I know him intimately. Free Life depends on this anchor of intimacy built on trust. Trust comes from faithfulness of walking together and getting to know one another. Men/women fail us often in life; trust gets broken by their choices to put themselves before us.

But God has proven through Jesus' sacrifice that He will not fail us. He passed the ultimate test. He was put to death on a cross, despising the shame thrust upon Him. He took on our unfaithful ways as those who intimately walked with Him betrayed Him and yet He chose to follow through for our freedom. He did not want us subject to the ways of mankind. He offered his life as an atonement for sin because the weight of trying to obtain the law code was untenable. He gave His life to break the bondage of the law code mentality. Think. Moses was not raised in slavery but in a palace because God wanted him to have a mindset of power and authority not a mindset of bondage. This was the way to break the cycle of slavery. We grow up in a mindset of bondage to the ways of society but God sent His son so that we may live freely in Him. It's not about whether you choose to drink, smoke, etc. It's about what you chose to do with Him. Are you walking in a real relationship with Him where you have given Him all of you? Are you willing to lay down your own hopes, dreams and future to follow His? He has a better place, the best place for you in your career, your relationships, your home, your future, etc. but you must be willing to put it all into His keeping. Freedom isn't about giving up or giving in to another. Freedom is defined as the ability to act or do without constraints. When your mind is stuck on following a certain set of standards due to constraints, that is bondage. Freedom is a choice. As a citizen of The United States of America, I choose to accept the laws. I choose to be a part of the place I live by the actions I take. I choose to be a Christian by choosing to fulfill the law of Christ. Free Life is not a life without anchors that hold us steady. Free Life is the choice to anchor. I choose to anchor in Jesus. He has proven worthy of my trust. He gave His life for me. I choose daily. I choose intimacy with Him. I choose a relationship with Him. I choose. This is the ultimate gift that God gave us. Free Will. The ability to choose Him. He loved us first and then gave us the ability to choose Him. Don't be fooled. You are choosing if you choose not to follow Him. You are choosing if you go your own way. You are choosing if you don't read His word. You are choosing if you don't go to fellowship with other believers. You are choosing.

His Chosen people are ALL who walk in Him by choice not by law, blood, location or religion. This is the boast of the cross. He chose the cross because of His love for me. I choose Him.

God bless you and keep you,
God smile on you and gift you,
God look you full in the face
and make you prosper.
In so doing, they will place my
name on the
People of Israel—
I will confirm it by blessing
them."

Numbers 6: 24-27

The Blessing!

Name dropping is a networking skill that lets people know who you know and makes you feel important because you are connected to important people. God was and is the original name dropper but the name he dropped is His because it is the most important! He told the high priests to say this over the people and by doing this they would place the name of God upon the people and He would confirm it by blessing them. Wow! Catch that! By blessing we are blessed! Jesus is our High Priest. He came and performed the blood sacrifice required to restore us to Him. He gave Himself as the spotless lamb and was lifted up in the air as required by Mosaic law so He could fulfill the requirements of the law that consecrated us before Him. In Luke 24:51, we see that the last thing Jesus did while on Earth as He ascended into Heaven was to bless the people as the High Priest of our lives. If Jesus Himself has put a blessing upon our lives through His sacrifice, who are we to doubt it? This is our weakness in that we doubt that God wishes to bless us, keep us, smile on us, gift us, prosper us, and look us full in the face! You cannot look someone full in the face without fully seeing them! God wants to completely see you and bless you! My sons know that I love a hug but they do not realize how important it is when I look them fully in the face. It is when I hold them close, looking fully into their face that my love for them overwhelms me so much that they could ask for anything and I would give it. This is how God is too. When we Turn our eyes upon Jesus and look Him fully in the face, we see His grace, mercy, forgiveness and overwhelming love. When we step fully into His presence and His embrace, we experience a fullness of joy like no other. All our fears and insecurities are erased and we are at rest. That holy hug is the blessing but too often we shrug out of it too quickly to fully experience the anointing and see the face of God.

Too often we are in a hurry and we rush through the moment of sacred blessings as we do brushing our teeth. It's just a rushed prayer, a hurry up so we can eat or get on with our day not realizing that the holy blessing of our day has been interrupted by our rush. We were in the embrace of our Savior but we shrugged out of that holy hug of prosperity because we were in a hurry to rush into the next activity. God created us with a need and value for that holy hug and physical ones too. Science tells us that oxytocin is often called the "love hormone," and it's released when we cuddle or bond. It's the reason why being hugged feels so good. Research tells us that when people hug for 20 seconds or more, the feel-good hormone oxytocin is released which creates a stronger bond and connection between the huggers. Oxytocin has been shown to boost the immune system and reduce stress. Hugs reduce stress by showing support. Hugs can help protect against illness. Hugs boost heart health. Hugs make us happier, reduce our fears, reduce pain, and help us communicate with others. All this from a hug and a look that becomes a blessing! I challenge you to step into God's embrace today. Accept looking Him fully in the face, feel His tender embrace and revel in His blessings to our lives. He so desires to connect with us by looking fully in our faces and hearts. His love is overwhelming for us and we see it, feel it and experience blessing when we step fully into His embrace. Then go bless another. Erase that spirit of criticism and negativity by embracing God and looking Him fully in the face. If you begin to speak Jesus instead of your words of doubt and fear, criticism and negativity, things will change. Struggling? Step into His embrace!

Speak the words of blessing over their lives as I speak it now over yours: God bless you and keep you, smile on you and gift you. God look fully in your face and make you prosperous. Grab them, look fully in their face and speak over them in loving prayer. Watch things change.

"Far-flung ocean islands see it and panic.
The ends of the earth are shaken.
Fearfully they huddle together.
They try to help each other out,
making up stories in the dark.
The godmakers in the workshops
go into overtime production, crafting new models
of no-gods,
Urging one another on–'Good job!' 'Great design!'–
pounding in nails at the base
so that the things won't tip over.

"Do you feel like a lowly worm, Jacob?
Don't be afraid.
Feel like a fragile insect, Israel?
I'll help you.
I, God, want to reassure you.
The God who buys you back, The Holy of Israel.
I'm transforming you from worm to harrow,
from insect to iron.
As a sharp-toothed harrow you'll smooth out the mountains,
turn those tough old hills into loamy soil.
You'll open the rough ground to the weather,
to the blasts of sun and wind and rain.
But you'll be confident and exuberant,
expansive in The Holy of Israel!

Isaiah 41: 5-7, 14-16

Bought Back!

One man's junk is another man's treasure or so the saying goes. We were not created from junk nor are we junk. Each of us is a precious and prized treasure created by the Master and in the process of becoming a masterpiece. The world and all of the "godmakers" are in panic as they see the end of times approaching but have only their hope to pull it together with their own hands. They have become so bold and brazen rejecting God and all His ways that He turned them over to a reprobate mind filled with horror and sickness which they fearfully cobble together, making up lies and stories filled with deception to try to polish their images. They keep trying to create a safe space for themselves because they and the demons of hell that inhabit them know that time is waning.

So easily they toss aside people as things to be discarded and used, from the unborn to the young child used in sex trafficking, to the adults used to prop up their agenda; all sacrifices on the altars of greed, power and government authority. But they know their time is fading and they will be held accountable for all they have done. They scramble like cockroaches at the light when the truth is told. What is junk to them is God's treasure and they have no concept. Collector items that are exceedingly popular one day become junk another. I love watching a piece of junk from a flea market or garage sale become a masterpiece in the hands of a visionary artist or someone who enjoys making new from old. It reminds me that though we are but dust, God creates us into masterpieces. He takes the matter within us and seeing our potential, He forms us into His image.

God doesn't make junk. He creates beautiful things but sometimes we trash ourselves with our choices and ways then He buys us back through His supreme sacrifice when we yield to Him again. Recently I went with a friend to a local flea market where she purchased the ugliest piece of a broken dresser I had ever seen. It was barely held together and had a putrid color to it. To me, that piece had served its purpose and was not even good for firewood anymore but to my friend, she saw potential. A few days ago, she posted a before/after shot and I was amazed. This piece had been redeemed from the junkyard, restored to purpose and renewed into a new work. It was gorgeous and I was shocked as I watched her hard work invested, sell for many times what she had paid for it. She saw value in the unloved, unwanted and broken piece. She put time, effort and love into restoring it and that investment paid off. My aunts have this same talent as I watched through the years and saw them restore homes and old pieces to new value. I have watched my parents and many others around me do the same with people that have been written off by others including our family. They invest in people who are broken, hurting, beaten up and used by life only to see that the true beauty of God's love through them restores what was said to be done and over, used up and cast aside. God created us then bought us back from the wages of sin which had given us a death sentence. We were a used up, worn out piece of nothingness propped up and nailed together but really just an insect of life. Worth nothing to others but highly valued by God because He sees our worth and has called us by name, we are chosen. He says, "I, God, want to reassure you. The God who buys you back." The Holy One of Israel is transforming you from nothingness to a useful tool in the kingdom of God. A harrow is a tool with teeth which is dragged over plowed land to break up clods, remove weeds, and cover seed.

God says He is using us to transform from nothingness-a worm-into a powerful tool of use by His hand. He says through Him we will become confident and expansive as we are used by Him. He will make the works of our hands have depth and value in Him. Through Him, we will be made more than conquerors. We have been bought back. We are in the hands of The Master becoming the masterpiece tool that He will use for His glory.

The fundamental fact of existence is that this trust in God, this faith, is the firm foundation under everything that makes life worth living. It's our handle on what we can't see. The act of faith is what distinguished our ancestors, set them above the crowd. By faith, we see the world called into existence by God's word, what we see created by what we don't see.
Hebrews 11:1-3

Firm Foundation!

It fascinates me that we as humans can accept the beauty and wonder of space, understanding that we are held to this round ball of matter by a concept of gravity and embrace the magnetic principles of the nebulous causing the aurora, but struggle to grasp the creator who called all of us into being by His Word. Each day I put my trust into chairs to hold me as I sit and a bed to hold me as I rest. They are both perceived foundations that I trust simply because I have laid or sat on them repeatedly with good effect. Since my back surgery, there isn't really a comfortable position so I must move around a lot throughout the night. I have learned what helps and what makes things worse by trying them but I rely on the firm foundation of my bed/recliner to be there when needed. How is it that we are so able to trust man made materials that have failed and had to be replaced in the past but struggle to trust in the One who created the matter these items are constructed from in the very beginning? One of my friends, Rajesh, takes magnificent photos of the night sky catching the galaxy through his camera lenses, seeing things we cannot see with our eyes because we simply do not focus as well. The beauty is there but we fail to grasp it because we do not focus on the details the camera and talented photographers do. Our handle on what we cannot see is finite. We cannot grasp eternity nor the things to come but we dwell in the minute, hour, time of our existence. The fundamental fact of existence is that trust in God and His love for us is at the core of everything we hold onto in life. We see the created and trust the creator. We see the chair and purchase it trusting that it is constructed well with the right material to last and to hold us. We see space and trust that we are held to this sphere by gravity that keeps us grounded. Our handle on what we cannot see comes from what we believe-our faith. If you have faith that God created the mountains, then you should have faith that He can move them. If you have faith that God holds you to the surface of this planet spinning in space, then you should have faith that He holds you in the palm of His hand. If you have faith that the sun which appears to go up and down really is a star we are circling as we spin, you should easily have faith that if God says it in His word, it will happen.

The truth is that the more we know, the less we trust. Trust in everything has been eroded in this day and age of technology because it can supposedly be fact checked or researched. If we trust so diligently to science, the big bang, evolutionary theory and such then why is it so hard to go all the way back...what created the collision of nothing out of nothing? The Word. He was the Word in the beginning and He still is. He came as The Word wrapped in flesh and He walked this planet for a time with us. He willingly laid down His life for us to show us the way of sacrificial living and authority. We have an example, a pattern and a course to follow. We know that He gave us power to overcome and He dwells within us as the Holy Spirit. This Faith is the firm foundation upon which we stand, sit and sleep. I rely on a firm foundation under my mattress to hold me at night. I grasp the principles of construction of that bed and those materials because I can see, touch and feel them. I believe that God created all that is in existence and this is what makes life worth living. The ACT of faith is what distinguished our ancestors. They didn't have all the science and yet they believed. Faith is an action. In the 11th chapter of Hebrews, the author lists a number of familiar examples of faith in action from Abraham and Sara to Moses, Samson, Samuel and David. By faith...I faith-I believe. I see by faith, I walk by faith, and I act by faith. By faith, everything under the sun is defined. We are either faithful or unfaithful, there is no gray area. We either walk by faith or by sight-it is a choice.

As Jesus left the house, he was followed by two blind men crying out, "Mercy, Son of David! Mercy on us!" When Jesus got home, the blind men went in with him. Jesus said to them, "Do you really believe I can do this?" They said, "Why, yes, Master!" He touched their eyes and said, "Become what you believe." It happened. They saw. Then Jesus became very stern. "Don't let a soul know how this happened." But they were hardly out the door before they started blabbing it to everyone they met.

Then Jesus made a circuit of all the towns and villages. He taught in their meeting places, reported kingdom news, and healed their diseased bodies, healed their bruised and hurt lives. When he looked out over the crowds, his heart broke. So confused and aimless they were, like sheep with no shepherd. "What a huge harvest!" he said to his disciples. "How few workers! On your knees and pray for harvest hands!"

Matthew 9: 27-31, 35-38

Heart of Harvest!

Confused and aimless describes the crowds of today as well as those of yesteryear that Jesus saw. Hungry and hurting, broken and aimless, lost and so very mixed up-this is the harvest. People are looking for hope! People are looking for real truth, a firm foundation and answers to the why of life. The unfulfilled dreams and wants eat at the soul and frustration mounts. In the ninth chapter of Matthew, Jesus is inundated with the needs everywhere he turns. He is constantly seeing these people needing help and he looks out and sees so much that must be done. His heart breaks because there are just not enough people wanting to be His hands extended reaching out changing lives. Too many in the "church world" of that day were so busy being hypersensitive and hypercritical much like today instead of being the heart of the harvest. Wheat doesn't become bread without a lot of processes. I read a little book when I was a kid about a hen baking bread. Everyone wanted the bread but no one wanted to help with the work though she offered the opportunity constantly to them. They wanted the blessings but not the toil. They wanted the reward but not the work. Jesus had gone to eat at Matthew's house serving the most in need. He had tried to reason with the Pharisees (the church world) but they refused to see. He had spent so much time helping and touching and honestly I believe He was getting exasperated. He was on His way home to rest and two blind men followed him into His house, so He asked them if they believed they could be healed and they said yes. Jesus touched them and said "become what you believe".

This is so wonderful because they did believe and they were healed completely. He warned them not to tell anyone but they didn't listen to the one who had just healed them from blindness! Then Jesus began to harvest. The heart of the harvest starts with belief. This whole chapter is about those who believed and spread the word of miracles. From the lady with the issue of blood who touched His garment, to the ruler whose daughter was raised from the dead, to the paraplegic man who began to walk, to these blind men-all had faith beyond sight. All of them believed despite what they knew. All of them were in impossible situations stretching out to the God of the possible. Jesus was the conductor of God's mission of love. He came and showed us how to love large and full. He came to give of Himself even unto His own death. His heart saw the harvest and called for others to join Him. This call still rings true. Jesus is calling us to be the laborers of the harvest. The bread is in the oven. The smell of warm love reaching out, calling those who are hungry to come near but someone must be willing to do the work. "Not I" said the duck, the goose, the rooster, the haughty, the proud, the I'm too good for that..."then you shall not eat of the bread" said the hen. Jesus is calling us to be a part of the harvest and to take part in the reward. What's your excuse? Are we harvesting in faith believing or are we one of those who will miss the feast because we are too busy with our own agenda in this temporal realm?

The fields are ripe. Your field isn't mine as mine isn't yours to harvest. God has placed you in the marketplace of ministry where you are. Yes, you may be fighting illness or other issues but there are people around you hungry, watching, waiting for answers. That nurse, doctor, other patients...what are you offering to them? That clerk, salesperson, drive thru person, waitress, stewardess, employee...harvest...see His heart. Be His heart of harvest and watch the windows of Heaven pour out over your life.

Help, God—I've hit rock bottom!
Master, hear my cry for help!
Listen hard! Open your ears!
Listen to my cries for mercy.
If you, God, kept records on wrongdoings,
who would stand a chance?
As it turns out, forgiveness is your habit,
and that's why you're worshiped.
I pray to God—my life a prayer—
and wait for what he'll say and do.
My life's on the line before God, my Lord,
waiting and watching till morning,
waiting and watching till morning.
O Israel, wait and watch for God—
with God's arrival comes love,
with God's arrival comes generous redemption.
No doubt about it—he'll redeem Israel,
buy back Israel from captivity to sin.

Psalms 130: 1-8

Forgiveness Habit!

Habits-we all have them. Some habits are good and full of discipline because they take care of us such as brushing our teeth and some are bad-which need to be changed! One habit we all have is whining and complaining. It's likely the hardest habit to break but the one that makes the most difference in our lives and in the lives of those around us. I've always heard it said that no one likes a whiner but since we all do it, I guess we all dislike it. David was a whiner and a conqueror. Lots of his psalms (songs) are a lot like country music with all the poor me cries but the difference is powerful. He cried out to God. He didn't go to a bar and whine to a bartender or spread his complaints through gossip on Facebook (or other means they had at that time). He complained and called out to God in song. Now, watch this! He starts at Help and ends at encouraging others within a few words! This is what happens when we take our complaints to God instead of to our neighbors. He learns the habit of forgiveness brings restoration. As it turns out, God taught him this while he was crying out for help. I'm sorry: Two very powerful words but more powerful than these is-I forgive! Mercy is God's habit of forgiveness. God's mercy is wider, deeper and more vast than we can grasp because we as finite humans have a hard time forgiving wrongs. God not only forgives but completely wipes away the sin as gone-He says as far as the East is from the West...like never ending forgiveness and clearance of sin. We as humans are at fault of forgiveness, but not forgetting of wrongs. We carry them in us and on us, bringing them up whenever some-one makes a mistake again. I challenge this. Is forgiving complete without the mercy of forgetting? Believe me, I know this is hard. This was put to the test in me recently. Someone who had wronged me years ago in a very big way walked into my office. I was blown away that she would even darken my door, but then I realized and caught myself. I was now the one in sin because I had not truly forgiven. I had just hidden the pain under the guise of forgiveness until I was confronted by it head on. I realized at that moment that forgiveness is connected to forgetting the wrong. This is hard!!! I know...I know...you want to give me all the excuses and reasons why forgetting isn't a good thing and that you can forgive without forgetting but I challenge you on this.

If you cannot embrace the one you forgave, figuratively at least, then you are still harboring the seed of unforgiveness which leads to bitterness. I've watched it in others and I saw it in myself. It wasn't pretty. I had to truly put it away with true forgiveness. I couldn't wallow in the things done wrong to me by them. I can remember my part in the situation so I will not repeat the things that led to the wrongful circumstances but if I hold onto the sin, I cannot embrace God's love which covers it. God's arrival fully into your life brings love overwhelming and generous redemption. We love the thought of that redemption for ourselves but what about the one who wronged us? Can we truly embrace mercy and forgiveness for them so much that we wait and watch for God to bring about change in their lives with bated breath? Are we able to move beyond the wrong into a place of true repentance and forgiveness? Can we embrace forgiveness as our own habit? Can we draw closer to the Source of love so much that His forgiveness and mercy become our lifestyle? I pray to God-my life a prayer-and wait for what He will say and do-waiting and watching. If God kept records, how vast and deep that record would be on us. He forgives and puts our sins away. "Let it go" is a song that became quite famous for a while as the fictional character broke free from her disciplined life into her own way of doing things but while she did, she wreaked havoc on all those around her. When we "let it go" with others, it shouldn't be a vicious self indulgent temper tantrum but rather a cry to the Almighty as David did. Scream out and rage, beg for God's help and cry but ultimately the path to true victory lies in the habit of mercy-forgiveness and forgetting the wrong. Maybe it is time to try a new habit-discipline ourselves to a new way-redemption from the hidden anger that erupts in our lives by creating the forgiveness habit. Consider this a challenge.

Waiting and watching-what will God do when I let go of that which has held me back by harboring the pain of old hurts-when I truly Let It Go? We are no longer the victims, we are the conquerors. We are no longer slaves to sin and unforgiveness but now we are overcomers. Yes, I embraced her. I forgave her completely though she never asked. Why? Because that is between her and God. God's mercy to me means that I can step into the light of His love and forgiveness when I embrace redemption which requires me to forgive also. The hold that wrong had on my life made me act in fear of it happening again. It limited who I was. With the arrival of God's mercy, I can truly say, I have put that past behind me and embraced my future. I will not hold onto past hurts or perceived wrongs but I will move into His loving habit of forgiveness.

The waiting and watching of freedom from the captivity of wrongs is over when we embrace His redemption.

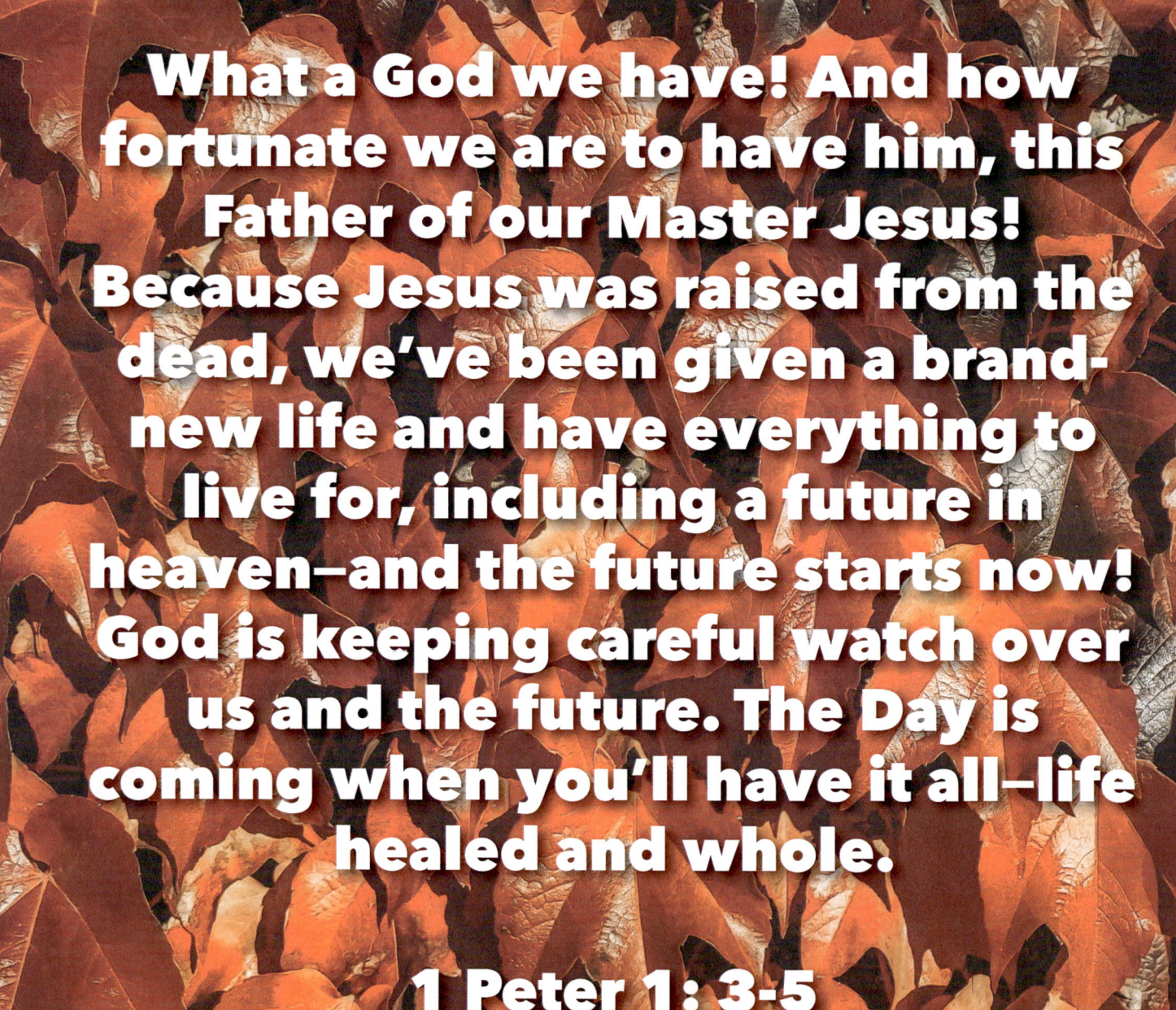

What a God we have! And how fortunate we are to have him, this Father of our Master Jesus! Because Jesus was raised from the dead, we've been given a brand-new life and have everything to live for, including a future in heaven—and the future starts now! God is keeping careful watch over us and the future. The Day is coming when you'll have it all—life healed and whole.

1 Peter 1: 3-5

Fortunate Future!

Back to the Future was a popular movie in my younger years because it allowed the character to go back in time to see things from a different perspective but in doing so small changes made to the past caused big changes in the present. Each thing we change about our lives, each choice we make affects our future though the choice be a simple one. A choice long ago made by Eve and Adam affects us still today but What a God we have that He redeemed that choice by laying down His life as a sacrificial lamb then being raised from the dead conquering the grave. Death has no hold on us now! We have been given a brand new future because of a choice we make to follow Him and accept His gift of love and grace that covers all our mistakes. As I visited with a young person yesterday and asked what they wanted for their future, the reply was I want it all. I thought, then I do too and I have it all through Christ Jesus. God has given me a brand new life and a hope for a future with a life healed and whole. That life starts now! That life includes a future in Heaven but God keeps careful watch over us now and He knows where we are headed. He knows our hopes and dreams. He has plans to prosper us and give us everything to live for when we put our all in Him. How fortunate we are to have Him, this wonderful Father of ours who is also the Father of Jesus. The small choices we make affect our outcome in eternity. We choose to accept Christ. We choose to lay it all down for His glory. I love the picture of the child with the broken toy (life) who gives it to God. The Master Carpenter repairs the toy and repaints it (in His blood) covering the flaws, making it like new so that the future is fresh. The choice is ours, to keep playing with the broken dreams or to give them to the Master. I still remember the day my son brought his little train to me and said, "Momma, my Thomas is broked, please fix him." His Thomas the train engine had a broken wheel and it was a simple fix for me but his little hands couldn't manipulate the tire to repair it. When I handed the repaired toy back, he said, "I knew it, momma fixes everything." My heart melted and forever cherishes that memory because the truth is that momma cannot fix everything but I know a God who can and I trust Him to give my sons a fortunate future. I know He will. I have seen Him work. He's the man who can fix it all no matter how broken. He makes beauty from ashes. He makes a fortunate future from dust. Whatever our broken dreams, He is waiting for us to call Him and give Him the "broked" so He can renew it into a fortunate future for us.

My response is to get down on my knees before the Father, this magnificent Father who parcels out all heaven and earth. I ask him to strengthen you by his Spirit—not a brute strength but a glorious inner strength—that Christ will live in you as you open the door and invite him in. And I ask him that with both feet planted firmly on love, you'll be able to take in with all followers of Jesus the extravagant dimensions of Christ's love. Reach out and experience the breadth! Test its length! Plumb the depths! Rise to the heights! Live full lives, full in the fullness of God.God can do anything, you know—far more than you could ever imagine or guess or request in your wildest dreams! He does it not by pushing us around but by working within us, his Spirit deeply and gently within us.

Glory to God in the church!
Glory to God in the Messiah, in Jesus!
Glory down all the generations!
Glory through all millennia! Oh, yes!

Ephesians 3: 14-21

Extravagant Dimensions!

Seeing a picture of an amazing place is neat and a video even better but experiencing it in person is so much more. I've seen pictures of the sequoias and watched videos online but when my family went and experienced it, that was amazing. A photo stimulates one's senses, a video too, but an in person experience tickles all five senses and more. To think that the Creator of the Universe carved the Grand Canyon and formed the seedlings that He knew would be these magnificent trees, is awe inspiring. There are many places in the world that I will never experience in person, though, just as there are depths of space I will never explore. We live in a finite world but we are not finite beings. Our temples of our bodies are finite and limited which sometimes is more evident than others but our spirit is transcendent. God has so much more for us than the limited plans and dreams of our current existence but we must grasp His purpose and His love in waves. A year or so ago, I took my staff to a 4D experience of Van Gough paintings. It was fascinating because all the senses were stimulated as the paintings formed around you and on you, surrounded by music and motion. The sensory experience was like being a piece of the painting and was a little overwhelming. This sense of depth, heightened awareness and length of infinity is what Paul is praying for the Ephesian people to experience, for Paul has been in a spiritual experience that took him to the length, depth, breadth and height of God's amazing love. He had experienced the walls of a prison shaking and falling open while he was singing praise to God. He had been shipwrecked, bitten by a poisonous snake and beaten for God, but through all, he experienced the overwhelming dimensions of Christ's love. As he writes, he says he prays for the Spirit to strengthen them in a glorious inner strength because he knows that strength of Christ living in him. Jesus Christ is the same as He was then and as He will always be. He doesn't give strength only to Paul or Timothy, He gives extravagant love of dimensional proportions to all of us but we must accept it. We must open the door wide and keep both feet planted in His love. In order to receive and experience something in person, one must take the journey. We must be willing to receive. Reach out and experience the breadth, test the length, plumb the depths and rise to the heights of His love. It is a fullness like no other. God can do anything much more than you could think or ask, God is the God of the impossible and He is God of the possible. His Spirit works within us, guiding us deeply, and gently to His full glory, so that we can experience so much more than we anticipate.

He is so much more than your wildest dreams. He has so much more for you than you could ask for or desire. He wants to bless you more than you could ever guess or dream. His love is boundless and unlimited. His knowledge is vast and undiscoverable by mortal men. He is so much more than our minds can grasp which is why no man lives who has seen God because it is more overwhelming than a sensory experience or a journey of a lifetime. It is beyond our ability to fathom but He gives us dimensions of His love as we are able to handle it. It may sound a little crazy but let's look at it from the perspective of Earth. There are many dimensions to Earth that have not been discovered from the oceans to the underground world. Each discovery is awe inspiring but these are only dimensions of a single word from God. The Earth was without form and void until God spoke. Singular words from God formed the vastness of all creation-"let there be light" formed the sun, moon, stars, galaxies, planetary systems, nebulas, vast space and so much more our brains cannot grasp but we see in photographs from outer space. He opens all of His thoughts and plans, abilities and experiences to us fixed in the extravagant dimensions of His love. It is time for us to go beyond ourselves and our own finite situations to see what He is truly doing, to experience the depths of His love, to embrace the future He has planned for us. We must get our minds off of the things that bind us to this limited world and see beyond into the heights of His abilities. He is so much more. He wants so much more for us. Time to move into the glory dimensions and away from the fixed mindset of loss and frustration that binds us into a mental load. We must set our focus on things above and not below.

Now I'm returning to you.
I'm saying these things in the world's hearing
So my people can experience
My joy completed in them.
I gave them your word;
The godless world hated them because of it,
Because they didn't join the world's ways,
Just as I didn't join the world's ways.
I'm not asking that you take them out of the world
But that you guard them from the Evil One.
They are no more defined by the world
Than I am defined by the world.
Make them holy—consecrated—with the truth;
Your word is consecrating truth.
In the same way that you gave me a mission in the world,
I give them a mission in the world.
I'm consecrating myself for their sakes
So they'll be truth-consecrated in their mission.

* * *

I'm praying not only for them
But also for those who will believe in me
Because of them and their witness about me.
The goal is for all of them to become one heart and mind—
Just as you, Father, are in me and I in you,
So they might be one heart and mind with us.
Then the world might believe that you, in fact, sent me.
The same glory you gave me, I gave them,
So they'll be as unified and together as we are—
I in them and you in me.
Then they'll be mature in this oneness,
And give the godless world evidence
That you've sent me and loved them
In the same way you've loved me.

John 17: 13-23

Consecrated Oneness!

Heart abounding joy is Joy complete in us. For joy to be complete, we must embrace the consecrated truth which is the word of God. The Word of God is a pure light that shines through the darkest clouds inspiring others to turn to the light. As Jesus prayed for the disciples, He was ascending from Earth into Heaven. While He is preparing to leave, He is instructing them through the prayer of John 17. He is praying to the Father to keep us in one heart and one mind in Him, so that the truth can be consecrated in us and through us, making us holy before God, so that we can become one with Jesus. The singular heart and vision is the evidence that Jesus is one with us. When we live in Him and His spirit abides in us, we can do all things in His name in confidence knowing that whatever we think or ask shall be done. The goal of this mission is the maturity of each one of us in Him, operating, working, serving, giving and living in a singular purpose for His glory. When a choir sings in one voice, you cannot distinguish the individual as it is so blended that it is perceived as one. Like a white light that is full of all colors, we are to be perceived as one with Christ. Only through the refraction and reflection of His light in us can the rainbow of color be seen. The sparkle of the diamond is the pureness of light passing through it. When there are cracks and crevices, the pure light is broken up into tiny rainbows of color. Consecrated oneness with Christ is when people see Jesus in us. In fact, it is when they see only Him and not us. When ourselves are glorified, He does not receive the glory. When He is glorified, we all receive the glory. Let me explain it this way. If you see only one color or band of the rainbow, you are missing the whole of the light. Your eyes eagerly track to see the rest of the rainbow and to see the whole. Rainbows appear as arches to us because of the horizon of the Earth when in fact they are circular. People in airplanes can see the whole circle as they are above the clouds which are refracting the light. Complete oneness is when the light passes through as a sparkle but is still seen as light, only more glorious. Jesus prayed not for us to be removed from the world but that we be guarded by God from Evil and not defined by the world but seen as one with Him. Jesus consecrated Himself through His sacrifice so that we can be truth consecrated to Him and through Him become sons and daughters of God just as He is. He gave us His authenticity and His authority to walk in, according to His truth. When we walk in His light, only He can be seen, not ourselves lest any of us should boast. Challenge yourself today to be consecrated through His word that others might see Him in you and be blessed.

Come, let's shout praises to God,
raise the roof for the Rock who saved us!
Let's march into his presence singing praises,
lifting the rafters with our hymns!
And why? Because God is the best,
High King over all the gods.
In one hand he holds deep caves and caverns,
in the other hand grasps the high mountains.
He made Ocean—he owns it!
His hands sculpted Earth!
So come, let us worship: bow before him,
on your knees before God, who made us!
Oh yes, he's our God,
and we're the people he pastures, the flock he feeds.
Drop everything and listen, listen as he speaks:
"Don't turn a deaf ear as in the Bitter Uprising,
As on the day of the Wilderness Test,
when your ancestors turned and put me to the test.
For forty years they watched me at work among them,
as over and over they tried my patience.
And I was provoked—oh, was I provoked!
'Can't they keep their minds on God for five minutes?
Do they simply refuse to walk down my road?'
Exasperated, I exploded,
'They'll never get where they're headed,
never be able to sit down and rest.'"

Psalms 95: 1-11

Stop, Drop and Listen!

Busyness is my secret weapon to keep my mind off the things which I do not like to handle. I learned busyness from the best, my mom. I watch her in her journey fighting cancer and in the worst times, she stays busy to keep her mind centered and not focused on things she should not. She activates faith in her life by going about serving and doing. I am all about the praising and raising the roof for God! I love singing His praises and watching the glory come down to lift the rafters because God is worthy; He's the best High King over all things. He knows us and cares for us well. Where I struggle is the drop everything part. We get so busy in life, doing, that we forget that resting in Him is important. Our sense of urgency about Him is not as prevalent as our sense of urgency about other things. I watch the hustle and bustle of this season in life and I am amazed that so few people stop to realize it is about Him and not the presents under the tree. David references a deaf ear as being the cause of God's wrath against His people.

Time and time again, He had to redirect their attention back to Him because they got caught up in the other stuff like worshiping other gods, making golden images, complaining that God wasn't good enough, whining that life wasn't perfect as if Egypt as a slave was better, etc. They just couldn't keep their mind stayed on Him for 5 minutes. Story after story of how they wandered away...the whole reason for their 40 years in the wilderness was because they couldn't believe the God who had opened the Red Sea to dry ground could conquer a few giants in The Promised Land of Canaan. We read about them and think-what's your problem? But then we do the same thing-get caught up in the who has and doesn't have, the I wants and the green monster of jealousy or coveting. We get frustrated by our lot rather than being grateful for each day. We look ahead in frustration because the road looks long instead of being grateful that the road has been made for us to walk. We get sidetracked by other things that draw our attention away from the One who is the all in all, then end up off the path following the feed of bait into the trap of the hunter. David's advice is much like that of the firefighters. When you are on fire, instead of running for your life which increases the flames, you should stop, drop and roll. When your life is in chaos and you cannot seem to find the right path, Stop, Drop and Listen! Stop what you are doing to stay busy. Drop everything to spend time with God-shut out all distractions! Listen to what He has for you! Listen! Remember the deaf ear was the cause of the wilderness journey. Listen! Take time to listen! Shout His praises! Sing Him songs! Bless His name! But most of all-quit complaining and take time to Listen!

Stop! Drop! And Listen! The key to opening the windows of Heaven and hearing from God is SDL!

Listen, Heavens, I have something to tell you.
Attention, Earth, I've got a mouth full of words.
My teaching, let it fall like a gentle rain,
my words arrive like morning dew,
Like a sprinkling rain on new grass,
like spring showers on the garden.
For it's God's Name I'm preaching—
respond to the greatness of our God!
The Rock: His works are perfect,
and the way he works is fair and just;
A God you can depend upon, no exceptions,
a straight-arrow God.
His messed-up, mixed-up children, his non-children,
throw mud at him but none of it sticks.
Don't you realize it is God you are treating like this?
This is crazy; don't you have any sense of reverence?
Isn't this your father who created you,
who made you and gave you a place on Earth?
Read up on what happened before you were born;
dig into the past, understand your roots.
Ask your parents what it was like before you were born;
ask the old-ones, they'll tell you a thing or two.
"Do you see it now? Do you see that I'm the one?
Do you see that there's no other god beside me?
I bring death and I give life, I wound and I heal—
there is no getting away from or around me!
I raise my hand in solemn oath;
I say, 'I'm always around. By that very life I promise:
When I sharpen my lightning sword
and execute judgment,
I take vengeance on my enemies
and pay back those who hate me.
I'll make my arrows drunk with blood,
my sword will gorge itself on flesh,
Feasting on slain and captive alike,
the proud and vain enemy corpses.'"
Celebrate, nations, join the praise of his people.
He avenges the deaths of his servants,
Pays back his enemies with vengeance,
and cleanses his land for his people.

104

Deuteronomy 32: 1-7, 39-43

Do You See It Now?

The song God gave Moses in his last hours on Earth is recorded in Deuteronomy 32. God knew His people would falter and fail. He knew that living on His promises would make them fat and lazy, unwilling to honor the God who brought them out, delivered them and set them upon the promise. He knew. He gave Moses a song to teach the people so that in His moments of wrath, they would remember His songs. His works are perfect. He is fair and just. A God you can depend upon with no exceptions is He. He brings death and life, wounds and heals, gives and takes away. He is God. He's always here with us, by His own name He swore for there is no greater. Do you see it now? He instructs us to talk to our elders, read the stories of the ancestors, and spend time in His word digging in to find His truths. The Rock never moves and His word is iron clad. He is the Father who made you, created you, and gave you place on Earth. Allow His teachings to fall like gentle rain, arrive like morning dew, and be perceived as the spring shower on the garden of life. Respond to the greatness of God. Embrace His fullness. Do you see that God is the one? There is no other like Him.

When I was a child, I saw God as the God of judgment who rewarded and disciplined as a parent. When I was a young adult, He was my source, my provider and the lover of my soul on whom I depended. As I have walked with Him for many years, He has become my confidante, my friend, my everything, my all in all but most of all my joy. He has been my healer, my counselor, my might, and my strength. He has been my lifter of my head in bad times and my anchor in rough times. He has been my meal when I was hungry and my dessert when I needed His sweetness to soothe my soul. He has been my intimate partner who sees me as no one else can or does. He has used me for His mercies and grace to others and He has been my mercy and grace through others. He has never left me even when I felt I was in a desert place; He was my oasis in that desert. He has held me, walked with me, comforted me, touched me, abided with me and just breathed through me when I had no words to speak. Do you See Him Now? Begin to look at your life and count the ways He has been there for you. From the accident you weren't in but might've been if not for that delay at the train to that provision just in the nick of time. He is as close as the mention of His name but He is so much more than you think or dream. He knows your need before you ask but He is a patient and gentle God. Don't get me wrong, He is still God and His wrath is hot and fiery. He is still a God of judgment both to you and to those who try to harm you. Listen Heavens; Attention Earth; here is a mouthful of words that declares God is God: Celebrate Jesus, Praise God, Worship the Spirit for they are three in One. Do you see Him now? If not, dig deeper. Your eyes may fail but His truth will not fail. Your strength may fail but His strength is enough. Your world may fall apart but that was never His plan to begin with, so put it behind you and move on into the newness He has for you! He is God.

Do you see it now?

Be prepared. You're up against far more than you can handle on your own. Take all the help you can get, every weapon God has issued, so that when it's all over but the shouting you'll still be on your feet. Truth, righteousness, peace, faith, and salvation are more than words. Learn how to apply them. You'll need them throughout your life. God's Word is an indispensable weapon. In the same way, prayer is essential in this ongoing warfare. Pray hard and long. Pray for your brothers and sisters. Keep your eyes open. Keep each other's spirits up so that no one falls behind or drops out.

Ephesians 6: 13-18

Indispensable Weapons!

More than words means to take action. It is application of the important principles of life. Paul instructs the Ephesians and through them, us, to be prepared as we are up against far more than we can handle on our own. God has issued weapons of warfare so that you can stay on your feet when the battle is the strongest. We must know how to use the weapons and apply them throughout our lives. The purpose of putting God's word into use in our life is that we are more effective at our purpose in the battle of life when we activate the weapons. The weapons found in His word are truth, righteousness, peace, faith and salvation. These are our armor and our guards as well as weapons against the fraud of the enemy. Further instructions are to pray long and hard-this is the true battlefield. Prayer is the turning point in battle and holding others up in their struggles. Encouraging others in the faith by lifting them up and keeping your eyes open for the deceitful traps of the enemy. Indispensable means that it cannot be replaced or substituted by any other means. An indispensable weapon is one we cannot live without. When Paul says God's word is indispensable, he is saying that without it, we cannot survive. The best advice or help you can give another is speaking the word of God over them. It is much more beneficial and more powerful than giving words of man/woman's wisdom. Learn that your opinion is only your opinion unless it is backed up by the truth in the word of God. We are a powerless and opinionated people without the love and truth of His promises and wisdom. Peace comes through salvation and faith in Him who made us. Clinging to His truth and striving for righteousness is action required to live. A weapon is useless if it is not with you and practiced. Prayer that avails much is prayer that is an action. Actionable prayer is as hard and long as warfare. It involves intercession for others and lifting others up in The Spirit. The action of salvation is the acceptance of the gift of Jesus Christ in oneself. The pursuit of righteousness is the result of relationship. The walk of righteousness requires the action of truth to steer us into the narrow path of faith. The action of faith directs us to peace, and peaceable action in our lives leads others to the prayerful acceptance of salvation through the example of Christ shining through us. Harness the belt of truth; put on the breastplate of righteousness; step into the shoes of readiness in the gospel of peace, cover yourself in the shield of faith, attire your head with the helmet of salvation and in all, carry, cite and encourage others with the sword of the Spirit which is the Word of God.

"If God gives such attention to the appearance of wildflowers—most of which are never even seen—don't you think he'll attend to you, take pride in you, do his best for you? What I'm trying to do here is to get you to relax, to not be so preoccupied with getting, so you can respond to God's giving. People who don't know God and the way he works fuss over these things, but you know both God and how he works. Steep your life in God-reality, God-initiative, God-provisions. Don't worry about missing out. You'll find all your everyday human concerns will be met.

Matthew 6: 30-33

God Steeped!

Preoccupied with getting and giving in this season describes the stress of most people. Instead of a time of thankful rest in His provision, we become much like the grumbling Israelites who whined about being tired of the manna being provided daily. Economically, looking around us, the stress is high because the dollar doesn't go as far as it used to go. The dollar store now sells things for $1.25 instead of a dollar which is just one sign of the inflation we are experiencing. Matthew is writing the words of Jesus down here as a promise and a checkpoint. Jesus is telling the people to relax and trust God. They too were living under a heavy tax burden with too much government influence-but theirs was captivity under the Roman government. Jesus was instructing them not to worry but to steep in God-reality and God-initiative. I attended a tea party the other night at a sister church and steeped in God. It was a time of refreshing and anointing while enjoying the company of sisters in Christ, who attend another gathering church weekly, than I do. The beautiful table arrangements varied from nativity to lights and there was delicious food and companionable conversation but most of all, it was about learning to steep in God. Sometimes our circumstances cause us to think we should embrace worry or stress rather than God. This is where we are steeping. A tea bag in the package is not spreading its fragrance and flavor but rather in the waiting. If that tea bag sits amongst the others and never is put into hot water, its flavor is never known. Its fragrance is never smelled and it has no ability to spread into other places. Hot water is what it takes to make our flavor and our truth known to those around us. I chose a Christmas tea which was full of flavor of cinnamon and other spices but a little bitter without some honey and sugar. As I put the tea bag into the water, the flavor began to be pulled from the dried leaves and the color of the water began to change. I worshiped along with my sisters, as I understood that our lives give off the flavor and fragrance of God when we are in hot water if and only if we were first shut in with Him to be full of God-reality and God-initiative. If we are full of ourselves, our tones are bitter despite the spiciness. We need the sweetness of God to be poured upon us as we steep in Him to become the beautiful cup of tea to be poured into the lives of those around us. If we steep in the waters of this world, our flavor gets pungent but bitter because we haven't taken on the fragrance of God. I grow mint. I love the chocolate mint, especially as it is so lovely a flavor. I have so enjoyed taking the fresh mint and making cucumber water and fresh mint tea. The flavor is astounding and refreshing while being so good for your belly. But the mint must first be crushed and roasted to get the flavor that allows it to steep the best. The mint leaf itself holds onto the flavor until it is crushed and roasted through unnatural means. Then it releases the fragrance and flavor it was intended to share.

Sometimes we wonder why God allows the crushing and the pressing, the roasting and the steeping. The reason is because His flavor that we are steeped in will release into the hot water places of our lives only as we are processed in His fragrance. If we do not learn to lean into Him in the crushing, pressing and steeping, our fragrance and flavor will not be as wonderful as He is. Don't worry, be happy was a popular song a while back. It's the song that traveled around the world and was lost on a world full of worry and stress. It could not take root because the world is full of stress. God calls us to be like wildflowers, unconcerned with who is seeing them but completely at rest in the presence of the Creator knowing that their beauty and time is all for Him. In His time, He makes all things beautiful and ready. People who don't know God fuss over the human condition and worry so much but we who know God are to be steeped in Him by being shut in with Him so that as the hot waters of life pour over us, His fragrance of peace and His flavor of confidence is released. He will supply all your needs according to His riches in glory. Time to get shut in with God in a secret place so we can store up His fragrance and flavor through the crushing, pressing and roasting. Lean into the process as He is working a good thing in you. A wildflower tea is a thing of beauty and fragrance. It blooms as the hot water is poured over it. It has learned that hot water is only an open door, not a closed exposure. It blooms releasing its fragrance and flavor while also showing the beauty of the flower. You are His. Become the wildflower of His glory by leaning into His gaze and steep in His glory.

"I've told you these things for a purpose: that my joy might be your joy, and your joy wholly mature. This is my command: Love one another the way I loved you. This is the very best way to love. Put your life on the line for your friends. You are my friends when you do the things I command you. I'm no longer calling you servants because servants don't understand what their master is thinking and planning. No, I've named you friends because I've let you in on everything I've heard from the Father.

John 15: 11-15

Mature Joy!

The secret is out but where is the line? When a store has a sale, they advertise and some of them have lines waiting to shop. The candle sale holds nothing on this! Jesus has given us the key to a joy filled life. The life of mature joy comes from loving others the way He loves us. He doesn't call us servants but He calls us His friends. He isn't hiding His plans from us but advertising them so we can get in on them and be a part. Joy is the purpose. Jesus said He told us these things for a purpose and that purpose is a mature joy. What is mature joy? It is the joy that the world didn't give and cannot take away. This joy that we have is all because of Jesus not because we got a great deal or finally achieved a goal. I have happiness a lot from accomplishment, but Joy is more. I am happy because my son is graduating college and my husband is accomplishing something he has desired. I am happy because I am filled with things accomplished. Happiness plus peace of mind equals the joy of living but you have to add perfect love to that to equal mature joy. Mature joy doesn't come and leave. It isn't driven by circumstances or seasons. Mature joy is confidence in the supreme love of the Master as your friend. Most people think of maturity as independence. They think that once someone begins to be able to manage something on their own, they have matured. Mature actually means fully grown having reached an advanced stage in the process. Mature doesn't mean arrived, complete or accomplished. It means moving from the beginning stage to the advanced stage. I know lots of adults who are less mature than my kids were at 3! Maturing doesn't come with age, independence nor responsibility though I hear that all the time. When students at my office become better thinkers or readers, one of the things I hear parents say is that they gained confidence or maturity. Parents see this in them because they are able to do more. When they move into more independence and more ability, the obvious growth leads to a natural comment of maturity as they conduct themselves more confidently. Skill, not will, led to that confidence. Exercising faith in the love of the Lord leads to a confident happiness in Him that others perceive as maturity and is defined in scripture as Joy. Joy is an inner feeling which is reflected as happiness which is more of an outward expression. Joy endures through hardship and trials but connects in Christ with meaning and purpose. A person pursues happiness but chooses joy. Our joy isn't complete outside of Jesus as He is the center of our joy-our confidence in Him no matter the turbulence. There is a story of an elderly lady sitting on a plane taking her first flight sharing with the one sitting next to her about it. When the flight becomes full of turbulence and the passengers around her are all in turmoil, they look at her sitting with complete serenity. So they ask why. She says, "I have complete confidence in the ability of the pilot because he is my son and he knows his momma is back here as a passenger. There is nothing he wouldn't do to keep me safe."

Supreme confidence in the unfailing love of Christ and exercising that authority of His friendship in our lives is what leads to mature joy. The world cannot give joy because they do not have it, no matter what product or service we sell. We can provide the best service and best skills but we cannot produce joy. We can bring happiness and accomplishment but Joy is only had in Jesus, Others, You. The most wonderful way to spell Joy is to get the order right. What a friend we have in Jesus with such love and sacrifice that nothing stops Him from giving us His Joy. Hebrews 12:2 states, "We do this by keeping our eyes on Jesus, the champion who initiates and perfects our faith. Because of the joy awaiting him, he endured the cross, disregarding its shame. Now he is seated in the place of honor beside God's throne." Jesus knew that He could endure anything for a season because the Joy was set before Him! He says in John that His joy is our joy. He took on the cross knowing that His act of supreme love would be the key to unlocking supreme Joy in our lives. When He was on the cross, our Joy was on His mind. He came so we might have life abundance! Grab this! Love like He loves! Put your life on the line for others! Give until you cannot give anymore! Be a friend of Jesus by doing all He commands. This Joy that I have is all because of Jesus!

"Don't bargain with God. Be direct. Ask for what you need. This isn't a cat-and-mouse, hide-and-seek game we're in. If your child asks for bread, do you trick him with sawdust? If he asks for fish, do you scare him with a live snake on his plate? As bad as you are, you wouldn't think of such a thing. You're at least decent to your own children. So don't you think the God who conceived you in love will be even better?

Matthew 7: 7-11

Conceived In Love!

I've read this scripture hundreds of times and even had God share nuggets of wisdom from it for past devotionals but I woke up with this verse on my heart in the middle of the night. God spoke directly to me through this verse just as He desires us to be direct with Him. We are so used to our dog eat dog world that we feel everything is a bargaining chip or a networking or scaling place. We forget who God is and get fixated on our situation so that we begin bargaining with God. God, if you will do this or that then I will do whatever we think that God wants from us and we miss out completely. Our own parents or we as parents are not as infused with love for us as He is. He didn't just give us love. He conceived us in love. Most of us know the process of procreation and conception involves an intimate act but few realize that before that act ever happened for your conception, God provided that spark. It's odd to contemplate that my children were carried in me while still in my mother's womb before my birth. The birth of my children required the eggs that were formed in my body while I was yet unborn to this world. God designed an amazing process of incredible balance in procreation. The eggs that would become my sons were present in my body when my mother was expecting me at around 20 weeks gestation so by the time my mother knew she was carrying a child, my future children were already planned. Think of this. It's mind boggling! God's plans are in play long before you were created by the intimate act of procreation. We were conceived of God years before our biological parents ever met!

This is not a last minute, oh you need something? Kind of God. He planned our lives and knew us intimately long before we knew ourselves. Why then do we believe that God is a trader of favors rather than a doting parent? Because we are flesh. We like our own way of things. We want to manipulate the plan to our own making and desires when He sees so much more for us. I do not have a daughter this side of Heaven so I never carried my grandchildren but God knew this. He conceived us in love. Conceived by definition starts as a thought. We are a God thought before we are. We were conceived by Him in love before the creation of time. I know...our minds cannot grasp this fully because our brains are finite and time-bound, but try. The God of infinity thought of you before the creation of the world and put the things in motion that concern you today. If He so intimately conceived you in love in the details of who you are, then why worry? He's got this. Be direct with Him about your feelings and thoughts, needs and emotions for He knows you more intimately than any other. He knows that cell popping up out of control and misbehaving, called cancer in your body. He can speak to that cell and He can give wisdom to doctors to direct your health. There are no surprises to Him. This life is not a shell game where God is constantly moving the rewards so you cannot have them nor is this a trick or deceiving plan. God has His eye on us. His heart is set on us being with Him, in Him, complete and full of Joy. He desires the best for us. He isn't worried about our tomorrow because He knows it. He isn't worried about our troubles because He knows the solution. God, you know my need before I even ask but I also know it pleases you for me to ask. Lord, I need your wisdom and provision in the situations in my life.

This is how we know we're living steadily and deeply in him, and he in us: He's given us life from his life, from his very own Spirit. Also, we've seen for ourselves and continue to state openly that the Father sent his Son as Savior of the world. Everyone who confesses that Jesus is God's Son participates continuously in an intimate relationship with God. We know it so well, we've embraced it heart and soul, this love that comes from God.

1 John 4: 13-16

Deep and Steady Life!

I'm a hugger. I love a deep, steady hug because it conveys feelings of heart and soul. Not everyone likes to hug and especially with all the changes in our world since Covid. People are less intimate and more sedate in their approach to others. Life gives life. When we confess Jesus is God's son, it is a stance to the world that requires a continuous intimacy with Him. Embracing what we believe wholeheartedly is how people know we are sincere and passionate. Intimacy in a relationship is evident in a hug. When I was younger, I traveled a lot to other countries to visit. When in Rome..well, you do as that country's people do. In France, people openly kissed as a greeting which was a shock for the students who traveled with me. Some were very open to embracing but the whole kissing as a greeting really threw them. Their sense of intimacy was affronted and they wanted nothing to do with the practice. It was easy to identify who was from which country because the level of intimacy was very different. When we are deeply involved in a steady relationship, it isn't hard to see the intimacy and feel it surrounding people. John had walked in an intimate relationship with Christ Jesus. He knew Jesus deeply and personally. He was martyred for his belief in Christ. Jesus' life force lived intimately in John from His very own Spirit. Jesus has given us that same Spirit that raised Him from the dead to live in us. The deepness and intimacy of our spirit with His is evident in our daily walk. I am ashamed to admit that very often I forget who I represent and allow my own spirit of fleshly thoughts and desires to take precedence. It is evident by our behavior, our words and our deeds who we reside in and who lives in us. Yesterday, I saw a post on social media blasting someone that I think a lot of and it hurt me. I could not fathom the description of that person by this lady because that is not the person I know. My perception was that surely they must be mistaken because I know this person and the description did not align with what I knew of them. This is what I mean about intimacy. If someone says my husband did or did not do something, I know immediately if they are telling the truth because I know him intimately. This is God. God wants us to be so intimately connected to Him that we walk in a deep and steady hug. His Spirit lives in us and we know instantly if something is of God or not because we know God. His very life breathes in us and through us. His breath is our breath. When you breathe deeply in Him, His steady presence fills you and you are known by His name. People will know you by this.